THE BIOLOGY OF
AFFLUENCE

THE BIOLOGY OF AFFLUENCE

Edited by

GEORGE SMITH

AND

JOHN C. SMYTH

FOREWORD BY
LORD BOYD ORR

OLIVER & BOYD · EDINBURGH

OLIVER AND BOYD
Tweeddale Court, 14 High Street
Edinburgh EH1 1YL
A Division of the Longman Group Ltd

© 1972 Oliver & Boyd

ISBN 0 05 002354 3

Printed in Great Britain by
T. and A. Constable Ltd., Edinburgh

Contents

Contributors

W. Ferguson Anderson, OBE, MD, FRCP
David Cargill Professor of Geriatric Medicine, University of Glasgow.

Sir Dugald Baird, MD, DSc, LLD, FRCOG, DPH, RCPS
Emeritus Professor of Obstetrics and Gynaecology, University of Aberdeen.

Kenneth L. Blaxter, PhD, DSc, FRSE, FRS
Director, Rowett Research Institute, Bucksburn, Aberdeen.

Rt. Hon. Lord Boyd Orr of Brechin, CH, DSO, MC, MA, DSc, MD, LLD, HFIBiol, FRS, FRSE
Chancellor of Glasgow University; Nobel Peace Prize 1949; late Director General of FAO; former Director of the Rowett Research Institute, Aberdeen.

Sir David P. Cuthbertson, CBE, MD, DSc, LLD, Dr.h.c, FRCPE, Hon. FRCSE, Hon. FRCPath., FRSE
Hon. Senior Research Fellow in Pathological Biochemistry, Department of Pathological Biochemistry, University of Glasgow and Royal Infirmary; formerly Director, Rowett Research Institute, Aberdeen.

H. John Evans, BSc, PhD, FRSE
Hon. Professor, University of Edinburgh; Director, MRC Clinical and Population Cytogenetics Research Unit, Western General Hospital, Edinburgh.

Robert C. Garry, MB, ChB, DSc, FRSE, FRCP
Emeritus Professor of Physiology, University of Glasgow.

John Hawthorn, BSc, PhD, ARCST, FRIC, FRSE
Professor of Food Science, University of Strathclyde.

Magnus Pyke, BSc, PhD, FIBiol, FRIC, FRSE
Manager, Glenochil Research Station, Menstrie, Clackmannanshire.

Robert L. Richards, MD, FRCP
Consultant Physician, Western Infirmary, Glasgow.

George Smith, MBE, DSc, MD, FIBiol *(editor)*
Regius Professor of Surgery, University of Aberdeen.

John C. Smyth, BSc, PhD, FIBiol, FLS *(editor)*
Head of Department of Biology, Paisley College of Technology.

J. Ian Waddington, LRIC, MIBiol, PAIWE, MInstWPC, MInstPHE
Director, Clyde River Purification Board, East Kilbride.

Robert E. Waller, BSc, ARCS
MRC Air Pollution Unit, St. Bartholomew's Hospital Medical College, London.

Foreword

These interesting and informative papers form an important addition to the growing list of publications by scientists on the grave problems of today's world. They should be studied against the background of the great new powers science has given us.

The physical sciences have given us nuclear and chemical weapons which increase the capacity to kill. The biological sciences have given us the conquest of disease and the knowledge of how the world food supply could be doubled. The application of these brings life and health. Since 1900 the average length of life at birth in countries where they have been applied has increased by twenty years.

One of the papers defines affluence as that state of society where the materials and facilities necessary for health and happiness are available in abundance. More than half the people in the world do not enjoy this affluence which could be made available to all the people at a tenth of the money spent on weapons and other things needed for a war.

The world today is faced with the alternative of conflict of governments with death and destruction, or co-operation for life, health and happiness for all mankind.

The future depends on the youth of today. I commend this book of papers by eminent biologists to students of universities and secondary schools.

BOYD ORR

Introduction

This slim volume consists of a series of essays by a group of scientists, each expert in his particular subject. It originated in a symposium held in 1969 in the University of Aberdeen, organised by the Scottish Branch of the Institute of Biology.

The somewhat ambitious title of *The Biology of Affluence* will make it immediately obvious that cover of our subject cannot be other than partial. The state of affluence, with its overtones of population increase, rapid environmental change and resultant damage to living systems at every level from bacterial to human, has become the subject of public anxiety. Much recent comment has been concerned with the far-reaching effects of these changes on the biology of our environment. In preparing this book we have therefore chosen to look at the state of affluence more through its effects on the biology of the human beings exposed to it. With this point of view in mind, we have invited a panel of experts to illustrate the subject each from his own particular area of expertise. This has the virtue of bringing an interdisciplinary approach into a sphere where it is badly needed. Gaps there will inevitably be, but by use of the references and suggestions for further reading at the end of each chapter, we hope that large areas only cursorily touched on, or even omitted, can be further explored by the interested reader.

For the purposes of this book the definition of affluence has been agreed as 'that state of societies or of individuals in which materials and facilities are available in excess of those necessary for the maintenance of physical and psychological health'. Our contributors explore many ways in which this state of affairs has raised problems of disharmony between modern man, still biologically adapted for the conditions in which his ancestors evolved, and the much altered circumstances which he himself has created.

In the last three decades of this twentieth century the world population, barring an atomic or some more obscure cataclysm, may reach 6,000 million souls. It is, therefore, timely for all sentient citizens to think deeply about what the affluent society is really to be, and then to act, each to his or her full powers, to meet the increasing challenges of food production, population limitation and cessation of environmental contamination.

If you, the reader, ponder these aspects of life today, as we are sure these chapters will encourage you to do, then this publication at least will have merited its production.

We owe a particular debt of gratitude to Lord Boyd Orr for contributing a foreword to this book, and it was with much regret that we learned of his death while it was in preparation for the press. It is singularly apt that he, as the first director of the Rowett Research Institute, Aberdeen, should preface this book which contains essays by his two immediate successors. Furthermore, the unifying theme of these chapters might be said to correspond with his life's work, dedicated to ensuring an equilibrium between man and his environment.

THE EDITORS

R. C. GARRY

Man and his environments

If an animal is to survive it must be in harmony with its environment. Such harmony is achieved, according to conventional biological thinking, by the animal adapting itself to its environment. The more successful the adaptation the greater the chance of survival. On this view the environment is dominant, the living animal must conform or perish. As a corollary, the animal is powerless to alter the environment.

In past ages human beings were also in this situation. Modern civilisation has brought about a dramatic revolution in man's circumstance—a revolution or a catastrophe? Human beings no longer live dangerously at the mercy of an uncontrolled environment. Civilised man has taken a grip of his environment to mould it, wisely or unwisely, to his desires. And man is not content to lord it over his external environment alone. There is an internal environment within his own skin which he is now beginning to understand and to be able to modify.

This knowledge of, and this power over, our environments ought increasingly to give human beings the materials and facilities necessary for physical and mental wellbeing. But in the event, how is it with man?

We dwell in two worlds: these are our *external* and *internal environments*.

There is the rumbustious *external environment* of sunshine and storm with wild fluctuations of physical circumstance: there are extremes of climate and widely different geographical terrains. The mode of life may vary from the primitive pastoral to the sophisticated agricultural; and now we have the monstrous conurbations of modern civilisation with foul pollution of the air we breathe.

How very different is the peace and quiet of the *internal environment*: here is relative stability. At most there is the gentle

1

ticking of negative feedback. Our bodily processes hunt about an acceptable mean which ensures homeostasis of the real world in which we live, the world within our skins.

Claude Bernard said:

> 'La fixité du milieu intérieur est la condition de la vie libre.'

Stability is a better word than fixity, and this stability is very highly developed in man. Primitive man had this stability, and so managed to wrest comparative freedom from his physical surroundings, surroundings over which he, at that time, had little control. But it was a precarious freedom. The main source of energy which our forefathers could tap came from skeletal muscles, those of draught animals and of their own bodies. Their bodies were adapted to a life of muscular toil. Food had to be won by hunting or by labour in the fields. Even then the supply was uncertain, there were seasonal variations outwith man's control and, on occasion, wasteful glut or downright famine.

The elaborate processes of alimentation, digestion and absorption of food were adjusted to consumption of large quantities of victuals in a raw and crude state. Health, and life itself, were menaced by other members of the living creation, animal and human. The body of primitive man was for ever tuned to fight or flight. And he was certainly parasitised, both inside and out, by various forms of lower life. If attacked by micro-organisms his only chance of survival lay in development of immunity within his own body, in his own internal environment.

Yet man, as a biological species, although not as an individual, was in the safe keeping of his power to maintain the integrity of his body, often for a rather limited span of years, in the face of a hostile environment. He was usually able to breed fast enough to counteract the lethal effects of pestilence and of catastrophe. In the long, drawn-out grey dawn of pre-history, and indeed until very recent historical times, human beings had little or no control over their physical surroundings. They were pathetically powerless little creatures. But how conceited they were, quite sure that they were a special creation!

Now at last we human beings have begun to justify this

arrogance and conceit. We are now reaching out to take control of our external environments.

At the present this control is far from complete, but, for good or ill, we, for the first time in history, have very considerable power over our physical surroundings. And the plant and animal kingdoms are also being dragooned to serve our human needs. This major change in human circumstance has come about literally within the last few years. And it is an accelerating process.

We are, moreover, not content with domination over our external environment. We are now rapidly learning about the processes within our internal environment and are beginning to meddle there too.

In spite of our meagre knowledge and limited powers we yet venture to interfere with our physical surroundings and with the delicately-poised biological organisms which are ourselves. We face the difficulty that our internal environment is biologically ancient. Our homeostatic physiological processes are primarily adapted to deal with stresses from an environment to which urbanised civilised man is no longer exposed. We have neither built-in processes to deal with the external environment of modern civilisation nor homeostatic processes to protect us against fiddling interference with our internal environment. We lack factual knowledge, our understanding is defective and we are not wise.

Imbalance between our ancient physiological make-up and a man-made external environment appeared first when man deserted the land for the town and city. In ancient and in mediaeval times knowledge was lacking and power was trivial. The early communities of man must have been a welter of malnutrition, ill-health and pestilence.

Now, however, we have some knowledge of physiology and of pathology: we have considerable power. There are tremendous possibilities for good. If production of proper food keeps pace with growth of population, if preservation and transport of food is efficiently organised, then malnutrition and the horror of famine ought to be scourges of the past.

But our present-day alimentation is that of our ancestors before the impact of civilisation, above all, of urban civilisation. We have the stomach, intestines and appetites of our forebears who earned their daily bread by physical toil. We crave for food in bulk, and in physical nature, very similar to the food our ancestors ate.

Otherwise our gut does not function properly.

If we eat, digest and absorb food, in nature and quantity geared to our primitive alimentary canal then we 'import' far too much energy. 'Export' of energy by muscular work is far less than the 'import'. We burn petrol in the internal combustion engine instead of carbohydrate in our muscles. The balance appears in our bodies as fat. Obesity is truly malnutrition since obesity threatens life. There is no more typical disease of affluent society. Nutrients are available in excess of what is adequate for health and the machine takes the place of muscular effort.

It is terribly difficult to cope with this imbalance. Desire for food is a very natural appetite. But need we pander quite so blatantly to this appetite by excessive respect for the gourmand? If we have the sense and fortitude to restrict our intake of food we are apt to throw our digestive processes out of gear. Bluntly, our digestive system is an anachronism in this brave new world of machinery and of affluence.

There is another most interesting example of disharmony between our archaic internal environment and our modern external environment. This example, too, illustrates remarkably sloppy thinking about man's modern estate. Human beings are homoiothermic: that is, in health, the temperature of our body is remarkably steady. If our surroundings are cold, quite automatically, and without taking thought, we adjust ourselves to conserve body heat; if the cold is severe we shiver and so make additional heat to counteract the cold. On the other hand, if our surroundings are warm, changes automatically take place in us to remove heat and to reduce production of heat.

All textbooks on Physiology describe these elaborate and most interesting processes in considerable detail. But it never seems to occur to the learned authors of these texts that modern man has quite other ways of stabilising the temperature of his body. The automatic, physiological, stabilising processes, however efficient, could never enable us, as we now can, to live in some comfort at the South Pole!

We are not just another type of vertebrate animal: we are

very special animals, we have power backed by knowledge. We weave new fabrics, we design suitable clothes, we heat our dwellings. All the year round, wherever we may be, we affluent folk tend to live in a congenial subtropical climate, sometimes known as the Hollywood climate.

Is this wise of us, is this good for us? In an equable, pleasantly warm climate we lose our inborn power to cope with reasonable extremes of temperature. There is considerable evidence that, when we live in an enervating, controlled, sub-tropical climate we become physically flabby. We would probably be healthier, and feel happier, were we not so much in control of the temperature of our surroundings.

Fortunately, our inborn powers to deal with reasonable degrees of warmth or cold are not gone for ever. By graded, repeated exposure to heat or cold we can regain our primitive powers. This is the process known as acclimatisation.

It is not fair, however, to imply that we, with increasing power over our surroundings, always lay traps for our unwary footsteps. Power, used with intelligence, ought to be for our benefit. Wise use of power enables us to fly in safety at altitudes which would be fatal in seconds to human life: space flight is an even more dramatic extension of such knowledge and power.

In our nicely balanced internal environment we are also facing problems. We have again rapidly increasing knowledge with consequent power and control.

Not so long ago interference with our internal environment was limited to the empirical use of drugs. The use of alcohol, of tobacco, of drugs of addiction is a relatively ancient social practice. The physician floundered about with Galenical preparations and a wealth of purgatives. Medical practice, due to ignorance, was far from rational: the wise physician frequently fell back on *vis medicatrix naturae*.

When our bodies are invaded by micro-organisms or viruses, our cells make antibodies to kill the invaders or to neutralise the toxins. If we recover, these antibodies usually remain in us to the end of our days so that we rarely suffer from a second attack by the same disease. Human beings were astute enough, quite early on, to make use of this power by deliberate infection of susceptible people with mild forms of the disease. This was the forerunner of vaccination which brings about protection by active immunity. Later we learned how to confer passive immunity by injection of antitoxins.

Quarantine was a rational, cold-blooded device to keep infected persons outside the community. Quarantine has the grave weakness that the inhabitants of a community protected by quarantine are at risk of a major epidemic should the quarantine be breached.

The hope to discover a chemical substance lethal to invading germs and harmless to the host was realised by Ehrlich when he discovered salvarsan to treat syphilis. Now, of course, civilised communities have a wealth of sulphonamides and of antibiotics. The victim of an infection no longer has to produce antibodies to cope with the invasion of his body. His physician administers the appropriate drug to kill the invaders. But this does leave the individual dependent, as often as he is attacked, on the availability and the correct choice of an antibacterial agent. Germs, too, have an awkward knack of developing a resistance to our drugs. The physician may have hurriedly to ring the changes on his drugs to find an effective antidote to the bacterial onslaught. Indeed, it is a ding-dong fight between the germ on the one hand and the physician on the other. And this is so, even although the physician is backed by the knowledge and skill of the pharmacologist and the chemist. These three could well be worsted by the germ and then we would all need to fall back on our individual resources in the way of antibody formation.

Hardly a week passes, nowadays, without the introduction of a new drug by the pharmaceutical industry. In spite of the care taken by the industry, and great care is taken, unless these new drugs are used by the medical profession, and by the public, with circumspection there is danger. We now talk about 'iatrogenic disease', physician-induced illness: the thalidomide disaster is fresh in our memory. We are meddling with imperfect understanding in our internal environment. Again, until very recent years, we cheerfully exposed human beings to considerable doses of ionising radiations. We added carcinogenic colouring agents to cakes and probably still permit the addition of substances to food which may be harmful. It is too much to expect our internal environment to cope in every instance.

In the early days of the Royal Society there was a demonstration of transfusion of blood from one dog to another dog. Pepys, with inspired foresight, speculates whimsically on possible applications to man.[1] As he says, and in his own words

'This did give occasion to many pretty wishes, as of the blood of a Quaker to be let into an Archbishop, and such like.'

Nearly 300 years were to pass before we had the knowledge to make blood transfusion a safe commonplace in the manipulation of our internal environment.

Endocrinology is a relatively new branch of biology. Knowledge here has enabled us to intervene with ever increasing effect in our internal environment. Substitution therapy with hormones is rational and effective in many cases. An early instance was the dramatically successful administration of dried thyroid gland in myxoedema and then in cretinism. The dramatic isolation of insulin and its use in treatment of diabetes mellitus occurred in the early twenties.

A very lively issue at the present time is the use to which we put our knowledge of the ductless glands which control sexual activity. We have a 'fertility' hormone, use of which may lead to a disconcertingly large multiple birth. The hormones of the gonads may be used to prevent conception: could there be greater interference with the female internal environment? Surgical termination of pregnancy can now be carried out with little risk. There is no need to spell out the psychological, sociological and moral problems which follow on such interference.

Within the very last tick of the biological clock, as it were, surgeons have learned how to transplant organs from one person to another. Technical advances in heart-lung machines have made possible transplantation of living hearts. But how do we know that the 'donors' are beyond hope of recovery? The medical men in charge are faced with a problem in ethics, difficult and unpleasant.

There is another difficulty. A transplanted organ, unless from a uniovular twin, is a stranger in its new abode: the host makes antibodies and then rejection of the transplant commences. It is quite possible to diminish or suppress the power of the host to make antibodies. But simultaneously the host's power to make antibodies against micro-organisms is lost and the host, with his transplanted organ, must be shielded against attack by germs.

There is little doubt that sooner or later a way will be found out of this impasse. Then we must ask ourselves how much time we dare ask surgeons to devote to this aspect of surgery. What is the relative importance to the community, on the one hand, of repair of a rupture and, on the other, of transplantation of a kidney or of a heart? We shall have to be affluent indeed to spare surgical effort for all possible types of transplantation of organs. Are we, as a community, as a nation, prepared to work sufficiently hard to make such facilities available?

Now we have what is practically a new discipline, Molecular Biology. This is the preoccupation of the modern biochemist who 'studies biological systems at the level of molecules and atoms'. Molecular biologists are probing further and further into our internal environment.

For a considerable time we have realised that the chemical substances we call vitamins are essential for health. Not so long ago, in our ignorance, we failed to ensure an adequate supply of vitamins. Today we know the molecular structure of most vitamins, we can synthesise them. We understand the role of vitamins in the chains of metabolic reactions. Consequently we can administer them to ourselves to prevent such deficiency diseases as scurvy, rickets and beri-beri. Our knowledge enables us to compensate, clumsily perhaps, for many of the defects in our environment and in our way of living.

With this ever-increasing control over our environments what is the prospect for mankind?

We are healthier, many of the scourges of the past are gone. We can now combat so effectively many of the ills that flesh is heir to that we have reached a fantastic, ludicrous and also tragic situation. We seem to be our own worst enemies.

The Department of Health and Social Security each year publishes the Annual Report of its Chief Medical Officer, Sir George Godber. In the Report on the year 1967 Sir George says:

> 'None can read the U.S. Public Health Service Report on the "Health consequences of smoking" and retain any

doubt that the abolition of cigarette smoking would be the greatest single contribution to the improvement of the public health still open to us.'

And in the Report of 1968, which was published in 1969, Sir George devotes a whole section to the dangers of smoking cigarettes.[2] Indeed, cigarette smoking has been well called 'personal pollution'. A good second to this 'personal pollution' comes pollution of the atmosphere and of the environment in general.

Does this mean that there is little hope of further betterment of the human condition either by control of our external environment or of ourselves? In the future is improvement to be expected not by new knowledge and power, but by avoidance of such folly as the smoking of cigarettes?

It is indeed true that in spite of increasing knowledge we have made no progress towards increasing the span of human life: more people are reaching old age but so far we are unable to stave off the process of ageing. Three score years and ten seem to be what most of us can hope for unless we come of what is known as a 'long-lived stock'. Will it always be so?

The most recent breakthrough by the biochemists is an understanding of the way in which elaborate molecules are built up inside cells. It is now possible to picture how the molecules grow. There is no reason to believe that discovery at this cellular level is at an end. The biochemists will probably ultimately understand the nature and details of growth, and, as a corollary, the nature of malignant growth. How long will it be before we are able to control both, normal and malignant?

If we become able to prevent or cure cancer, what then? Would this mean a community saddled with an increasing number of helpless, senile creatures in physical and mental decay? If this is the prospect, there are those who believe that discovery of a cure for cancer would be a biological disaster.

If, and when, we understand the nature of growth we shall probably learn what is the nature of ageing. With such knowledge we may be able to slow down or prevent the onset of old age. Need our arteries harden or silt up with subendothelial cholesterol esters? Atherosclerosis and coronary thrombosis now approach epidemic proportions in what we call affluent communities. Surely a way will be found to prevent these curses of our present civilisation.

As we become older the lenses of our eyes lose elasticity; ultimately we suffer from presbyopia, the sight of old age. Already the biochemists are studying this ageing process in the lenses of our eyes. With the understanding of this process will there not ultimately come control?

Methuselah may be waiting in the wings to step on the human stage! And simultaneously, of course, it will be a land of the ever young.

This may be a fanciful picture in the immediate future. But we cannot deliberately discard knowledge acquired or renounce control over the two worlds in which we dwell. As a consequence we are already living dangerously. How ironical that knowledge and power may threaten disaster as ignorance and impotence never did.

Our one hope of survival is in enlightened use of our knowledge and power. Our fate will be determined by the intelligence, imagination and wisdom of man himself, on his humane vision for the future. How true the saying from *Proverbs*

'Where there is no vision the people perish'.

REFERENCES

1. *Diary of Samuel Pepys*. November 14th, 1666.
2. Department of Health and Social Security, 1969. *On the state of the public health; the annual report of the chief medical officer for the year 1968*, pp. 226-231. H.M.S.O., London.

K. L. BLAXTER

Affluence and agriculture

Keynes in his *Essays in Persuasion* distinguishes two classes of human need: 'those needs which are absolute in the sense that we feel them whatever the situation of our fellow human beings may be and those which are relative only in that their satisfaction lifts us above, makes us superior to our fellows'.[8] The industry of agriculture is usually regarded as being concerned with Keynes' first class of human need, through the production of food. Affluence is perhaps concerned with the second class. Certainly Western society has progressed far beyond what Galbraith[5] has called the 'economic tradition of despair' and deep concern with the means of providing the large mass of people with the bare necessities of food, clothing and housing.

Keynes' statements about needs reflect a much older empirical law in economic theory, devised in 1857 by Ernst Engel, which states that the proportion of income spent on food declines as income rises.[6] This is of some relevance to agriculture. The weightings used in calculating the 'cost of living index' in the United Kingdom, now more euphemistically called 'the index of retail prices', show that less and less of average income is now spent on food. In 1914 food was given a 60% weight in calculating the index, in 1954 the weight was 39·9% and in 1967 29·8%. Clearly the proportion of expenditure accounted for by food has dropped to half in a matter of a half century, and by nearly 25% in the last 13 years. Correspondingly the average man now spends more than twice as much on items other than food as he does on the food he eats. Fifty years ago his expenditure on items other than food was only 70% of his expenditure on food.

From some retail and wholesale prices given in Table I it is evident that in the last 13 years retail food prices have risen at a rate greater than have wholesale food prices, implying an increase in the relative cost of distribution. Table I also shows

11

TABLE I

Index numbers of certain wholesale and retail
prices during the last 13 years*

	1954	1962	1967
Wholesale prices			
1. All agricultural products (primary production)	100	97·4	104·2
2. Materials and fuel used in the food manufacturing industry (including part of 1)	100	95·3	105·6
3. Products of the food manufacturing industry	100	111·1	125·7
Retail prices			
Food	100	124·3	145·9

* Calculation of the increase in retail prices for food entails
moving from the interim index of 1948, through the index
commenced in 1956 and that commenced in 1962. Data for
1968 although in part published cannot easily be given
because the new (1968) classification includes 'meals bought
and consumed outside the house'. This reclassification is in
itself an indication of affluence!

Sources: *Annual Abstract of Statistics* 1968, 1962, 1954[2].
Studies in Official Statistics No. 6 (1966)[1].

that the wholesale prices of food have risen very considerably
faster than have the prices of the raw materials entering the
food industry, and in particular the prices of the primary
agricultural products on which these industries ultimately
depend. This implies that the fall in proportional expenditure
on food in the last 13 years, if translated into terms of the raw
material component, is considerably greater than from 40%
of total expenditure to 30%. If an affluent society still consumed
food more or less straight from the farm, processed and packaged
in the way in which it was so processed in 1914—that is before
the growth of our modern food industry had really begun—
then the fall in proportional spending on food would probably
have been from 60% of total expenditure to 10%. An example
for a food with a low income elasticity of demand, given in
Table II, illustrates the service component of food prices.

TABLE II

The price of the convenience of porridge in 1969

	Actual old pence/lb	Relative
Wholesale price of oats ex farm corrected for husk content which has been given no value	3	100
Retail price of oatmeal	8	267
Retail price of prepared and packaged 'quick' porridge oats	17	567
Retail price of 'instant porridge' (introduced 1968)	27	900
Retail price of 'oat crunchies' prepared breakfast cereal	60	2000

These changes in proportional spending have a considerable effect on the farming industry. It is only natural that farmers wish to share in the growing consumption of non-subsistence or luxury products. Farmers too wish to have fitted carpets, continental holidays, beautifully packaged convenience foods and the odd meal out in an expensive restaurant. Farmers are not simply producers, they also consume; they have needs and in particular needs of Keynes' second class. Classical economic theory states that in a free economy prices of farm produce will fall consistently.[9] People do not normally eat two breakfasts if the supply of food increases, as it does as a result of technological advance in agriculture. Too great a supply leads to a fall in price and marginal farms go out of production. There are many instances in the world of this operation of primitive economic forces, where land has tumbled back to grass and farming has resorted to a care and maintenance operation—to what farmers here tend to call dog and stick farming.

Governments in affluent societies, however, usually take some action to prevent farming poverty. The devices are many. They include the Mansholt Plan for the E.E.C. which envisages taking land out of production in a rational way. Restriction of the acreages of crops sown or of quantities sold is a similar process. Income parity schemes include not only loan support to farmers but farm price regulation, guaranteed prices for farmers, and consumer subsidies. Basically these are sociological measures to ensure parity of income for those who work by the sweat of their brow so that we can eat. Besides the sociological argument for government support of farming in these ways there are, however, others. In the United Kingdom such arguments are usually couched in strategic terms, in terms of foreign exchange saving, and in terms of the amenity that a well-farmed countryside can provide to urban dwellers.[10] The last two arguments have often been aired in recent years; few talk about the sociological argument.

The reaction of the individual farmer to a fall in price is to produce more if government provides some stability of price structure, or to produce the same amount at lower cost to maintain income. In a time of growing affluence absolute income becomes more important than interest on his own invested capital. More capital is invested in the farm business to maintain income parity, labour is replaced by machine and the whole production enterprise is intensified. In the United Kingdom the provision of capital improvement grants by government has further encouraged this process of capital investment to maintain income parity; indeed, some argue that our farming is now considerably over-capitalised.

Obviously a point is reached earlier by some than by others when the marginal return on capital as judged by income parity is not worth while. Retrenchment then takes place or, alternatively, economies of scale are sought by amalgamation of holdings. Then farmers become more understandable as economic beings for with change of scale capital investment and return usually become more realistic.

The primary effect of growing affluence on farming thus appears to be twofold; firstly, and in accord with economic expectation, certain types of land become marginal and then make but a minor contribution to output and, secondly, agricultural methods are intensified on better land—eventually to lead to amalgamation of holdings or their vertical integration. In affluent societies as exemplified by the U.S.A. and Western Europe it seems a justifiable conclusion that the fantastic growth of agricultural technology through the application of scientific methods is the result of the fact that the proportion of the average family's budget represented by primary products is growing smaller. By definition an affluent society is not a hungry society, yet there is a greater drive to increase the efficiency of its agricultural industry than there is in those underdeveloped societies in which agriculture is at the subsistence level, and people are undernourished. The feeling of moral satisfaction that many farmers had when considering the value of their labours in relation to the United Nations Charter, which states that it is the right of every individual to be free of hunger, has been somewhat tempered by the brute fact that farming in an affluent society can now meet these needs. Farming in such a context now caters not so much for physiological needs as for the legitimate desire for a more attractive and relished minimal diet.

It is pertinent in view of the last statement to consider what these desires are, and an indication can be obtained from income elasticities of demand. These state the percentage increase in expenditure on a commodity for a 1% increase in income. The overall demand elasticity for food in the United Kingdom is now about 0·2. This can be compared with values of 0·6 to 0·8 in developing countries and one of 0·92 for England in 1795.[4] Relevant values for individual foods are shown in Table III. Clearly with increased affluence bread and flour consumption decline, potato, sugar and jam consumption do not change, purchase of animal products increases about in proportion to total spending on food, while poultry and frozen vegetables are the new luxuries. The demand of a society growing in affluence is for more animal products and vegetables, and less of the older staple commodities. In addition, it clearly demands foods of convenience, a convenience more readily imparted in the food factory than on the farm.

I have dealt at some length with the effects of economic growth on the farming industry since these do much to explain current and possibly future changes in farming practice. They provide the context in which biological changes must be considered. We are currently dealing with the biological sequelae to changes in farming technology which are in large measure the result of economic pressures. These pressures in turn are themselves an inescapable part of progress of society towards a state of affluence.

The changes which British agriculture has undergone in the years since the Second World War are immense and are such that we now have the most technically advanced agriculture in

TABLE III. Some income elasticities of demand for foods
(percentage increase in amount of a food purchased for
a 1% increase in income)*

	Income elasticity of demand†	
	1955	1965
Items rejected with increasing income		
Bread	−0·05	−0·20
Flour	−0·20	−0·18
Items for which demand is static with income		
Sugar and preserves	0·06	+0·01
Potatoes	0·13	−0·05
Items for which demand increases with income		
Liquid milk	0·29	0·25
Carcass meat	0·31	0·25
Eggs	0·39	0·22
Items for which demand increases very markedly with income		
Broiler chicken meat	1·70	0·88
Quick frozen vegetables	1·72	1·22

* For comparative purposes obvious luxury items such as motor cars have income elasticities of demand of about 2·0, holidays and travel about 1·6 and household durables about 1·2 (Jephcott[7]).

† From National Food Survey 1955, 1966. The values are derived from cross-sectional rather than time-series analysis.[3]

the world. Measured in physical terms its output is prodigious. Few established British industries, if indeed there are any, can match farming's growth rate of 4% per annum over such a long period. Some of this growth has arisen from economic rationalisations; some has come from the application of science and engineering technology to the farming process. It is very evident, however, that the two causal groups of factors are not readily disentangled.

On the economic side rationalisation has led to increases in scale of operation, but these increases could only have come about to take advantage of technical advances. Thus, the grubbing of the boundary hedges of small fields was a step necessary to take full advantage of large farm machinery. The increase in the size of dairy herds was a step necessary to take full advantage of the labour economy introduced by the milking machine. Again, the current tendency to divorce crop farming from stock farming was unthinkable as long as livestock were an integral part of the maintenance of fertility on the farm. Now, with a deeper understanding of the nature of soil fertility, the ready supply of artificial fertilisers, and the means to assess the nutrient needs of crops, fertility can be maintained on many farms in the absence of stock. The development of intensive animal enterprises, the most notable of which are poultry enterprises, came about not because of economic pressures alone, but because technological achievements had provided a base for economic exploitation through knowledge of nutrition, husbandry, disease and parasite control. Similarly, the development of continuous corn growing enterprises came about not simply because costs of production could thereby be reduced, but because the advent of selective weed killers meant that such crops could be grown without problems of broad-leaved corn-land weeds becoming overriding.

It has been the combination of economic pressure and technical advance that has created the current revolution in British farming. Some may regret the disappearance of traditional patterns of farming, some may wish to conserve those traditional patterns; some fear what is new simply because it is new, or think that older patterns in some way included safeguards which have not been included in the newer departures. There is no reason to suppose that traditional methods have hidden virtues. After all, that tradition is not very old, for farming is incessantly changing.

It cannot be denied that technical innovations are not always sufficient to allow an economic exploitation. Each new departure results in the uncovering of new problems requiring new investigation. These constitute some of the most exciting and equally the most intractable problems in biology. Currently, continuous cereal cultivation is meeting problems due to soil-borne fungal disease, leading to investigations of new crop plants such as oil-seed rape to break and thereby control the cycle of infection. On the animal side we have a series of new problems engendered by monoculture in the form of diseases which under more extensive situations were rarely problems. The coccidial parasites in poultry which are now of economic importance are different species to those encountered when chickens strutted in the farm yard; many indeed were once regarded as rare inhabitants of the guts of wild birds.

Not all the problems are due to disease; some are more complex, and concerned with disposal of wastes. The problem of disposing of the dung and urine of stock housed intensively, at densities quite incommensurate with the size of the holding, is extremely worrying at the present time. An intensive pig unit can well produce as much effluent as a small town, and this effluent has to be purified if water courses are not to be contaminated. Even with silage-making effluent is a very real problem, for in terms of its biological oxygen demand it is far more demanding than town sewage.

Many of the sequelae to farming change have been foreseen, but some have not. In this regard Sir Geoffrey Vickers[11] has recounted the story of the man who fell off the top of the Empire State Building and was heard to remark on passing the 2nd floor 'Well, I am all right so far'. He used the story to point out the absurd speed with which we accept as normal unfamiliar things and the absurd slowness with which we appreciate any impending problems. These same points can be made about technological change in farming—readily accepted, but their implications slowly realised. There is a third point to the story which Sir Geoffrey did not make. A little more thought about consequences at the beginning can avoid rather a mess at the end. Happily we now realise more than we ever did before the importance of such thought.

Finally, I would like to return to the point or rather the paradox I mentioned earlier, namely the fact that the drive to increase agricultural productivity is greater in affluent societies than in those in which hunger is a reality. We have created a world of food plenty here in Western Europe; we can feed our 700 millions with ease, indeed we could feed far more if need arose. Starvation and under-nutrition are no longer real problems for we have fashioned the technical tools and acquired the new knowledge with which to make the earth yield more abundantly than ever before in the history of man. It is this new knowledge, these new tools of technology, which can now be used to help those less fortunate. The export of knowledge, of awareness of problems, of skill and expertise is undoubtedly the real solution to the fundamental paradox of our time, namely the co-existence of plenty and poverty in a bountiful world.

REFERENCES

1. Anon., 1966. *Studies in official statistics No. 6: method of construction and calculation of the index of retail prices*, 4th ed. H.M.S.O., London.
2. Anon., 1968. *Annual abstract of statistics No. 105.* H.M.S.O., London.
3. Anon., *Household food consumption and expenditure: 1966.* H.M.S.O., London.
4. Clark, C. and Haswell, M., 1967. *The economics of subsistence agriculture*, 3rd ed. Macmillan, London.
5. Galbraith, J. K., 1967. *The affluent society.* Pelican Edn., Penguin Books Ltd., Harmondsworth.
6. Houthakker, H. S., 1957. An international comparison of household expenditure patterns commemorating the centenary of Engel's Law. *Econometrica*, **25**, 532.
7. Jephcott, J. St. G., 1968. *Changes in household income levels and the demand for furniture.* University, Aberdeen. (Cyclostyled).
8. Keynes, J. M., 1931. *Essays in persuasion.* Macmillan, London.
9. Marshall, A., 1927. *Principles of economics*, 8th ed. Macmillan, London.
10. Prest, A. R., 1966. *The U.K. economy: a manual of applied economics.* Weidenfeld and Nicholson, London.
11. Vickers, G., 1968. *Value systems and social progress: the ecology of ideas.* Tavistock Publications, London.

R. L. RICHARDS

Affluence and the heart

As biologists, when we think of the human heart, we must forget all its romantic associations and think only of its physiological function as a pump. It is the most efficient pump ever known, maintaining as it does two separate circulations, with a stroke rate which can be raised in a matter of seconds from around 60 to 70 cycles per minute up to 140 or even more, and with an output which can be increased from around 4-5 litres per minute up to twice or three times that amount. Moreover, in most instances it continues to function efficiently without maintenance for the allotted 'three score years and ten'. Like all pumps, provided its initial construction has been sound, a break-down may be due either to failure of the driving force, to some internal derangement or to overloading. The medical counterparts of these mechanical events are congenital heart disease (faulty construction), valvular heart disease (internal derangement), hypertension (overloading) and coronary or ischaemic heart disease in which the cardiac muscle, which is the driving force of the heart, receives an inadequate blood supply and so fails to function normally.

If we now consider what effect the development of our modern affluent society has had on these forms of heart disease, we can find evidence that there have been striking changes in the pattern of valvular disease of the heart and of coronary heart disease since the start of the twentieth century, and it is on these two conditions, and particularly the latter, that I shall concentrate in this presentation. As far as congenital heart disease is concerned there has probably been little change in the incidence of this form of heart disease, but the technological advances associated with the development of our affluent society have enabled cardiac surgeons to correct many of the mechanical defects, such as 'the hole in the heart', which are the basic abnormality in children suffering from this form of

20

heart disease. As a result of such operations and with the control of infection by antibiotics plus the general improvement in standards of nutrition and child welfare many more children with congenital heart disease survive to lead useful and healthy lives in an affluent society. Hypertension (high blood pressure) remains. The relationship between hypertension and factors associated with affluence and the precise role of the heart and other factors in the haemodynamics of hypertension are not fully understood and for these reasons I shall not consider it further.

MORTALITY FROM HEART DISEASE

The best data that are available on heart disease come from mortality statistics. The condition which we now call coronary thrombosis or myocardial infarction, and which is the most frequent cause of death in ischaemic heart disease, was first described in the United States in 1912 and in Britain in 1925. Ischaemic heart disease, therefore, does not feature as a major cause of death before 1920. It is convenient also to consider that the development of our present affluent society has occurred over the last 50 years, and so if we look at the death rates from different forms of heart disease over the last half century this should give us some idea of the effect of affluence on the heart.

Tables I and II present some data on mortality from heart disease in Scotland.[1] It will be seen from Table I that there has been a dramatic fall in the number of deaths from valvular disease of the heart (mainly rheumatic heart disease) and a spectacular rise in those from ischaemic heart disease. Table II

TABLE I. Total deaths—Scotland

Year	Valvular disease of the heart	Ischaemic heart disease	Tuberculosis
1920	3,300	229	6,042
1940	2,482	2,613	4,003
1960	741	11,326	509
1966	689	14,472*	291

* This figure has risen to 17,798 in 1969.

B

shows how the proportion of the deaths from heart disease in males which is attributable to ischaemic heart disease has risen from 6% in 1920 to 75% in 1966. Although these figures refer to Scotland similar results could be quoted from most highly developed countries.

TABLE II. Mortality rate/100,000 males—Scotland

Years	Heart disease (all forms)	Ischaemic heart disease
1920-22	136	8
1940-42	366	80
1960-62	451	281
1966	449	335

The fall in the death rate from valvular disease of the heart can be readily explained as an effect of affluence. Rheumatic heart disease is a sequel of streptococcal infection, and improvements in the standard of living, better housing, better nutrition especially in infancy and childhood, better standards of hygiene generally and, since 1940, the introduction of chemotherapeutic drugs and antibiotics effective against the haemolytic streptococcus have all played an important role in this improvement.

It is more difficult to see a connection between the rise in the death rate from ischaemic heart disease and affluence. Certainly some of the increase can be related to such factors as the improvement in infant mortality and the fall in the death rate from infections like tuberculosis (Table I) which can be attributed to benefits accruing from our affluent society. As a result of these events more people are surviving to an age at which coronary artery disease is common. This, however, does not provide the full explanation for the marked rise in mortality from this form of heart disease.

If we look beyond Scotland at the international picture we find that most highly developed countries have a higher death rate from this form of heart disease than the so-called underdeveloped countries (Table III).[14] It is doubtful whether among these developed countries their ranking in the 'ischaemic heart disease league' is the same as that in the 'affluence league'. Scotland has the unenviable reputation of having the highest mortality from ischaemic disease but few, I suspect, would regard Scotland as a more affluent country than the United States and Canada, or even than England and Wales! Nor is the geographical picture quite as simple as it appears. As

TABLE III. International mortality statistics

Deaths per 100,000 population from arteriosclerotic and degenerative heart disease—1966

Developed countries		Underdeveloped countries	
Scotland	366·5	Venezuela	47·8
Denmark	327·7	Mauritius	46·5
Eire	326·1	Costa Rica	45·8
United States	320·0	Singapore	35·9
England and Wales	317·0	Mexico	16·9
Australia	290·0	Philippines	14·5
Canada	240·1		
Switzerland	218·6		
Netherlands	184·5		
France	81·4		

Professor Howe of Strathclyde University has recently shown,[3] if the mortality statistics are looked at in more detail it is found that they vary greatly from area to area. In Scotland for example the Standard Mortality Ratio* (S.M.R.) for coronary artery disease is 121 or over in the Clydeside conurbation, but is 85 or less in some rural areas in the west and northwest, and even within the City of Glasgow variations in the S.M.R. are observed; in the Provan and Ruchill wards the S.M.R. is 133 whereas in some adjacent wards, for example Cowlairs and Anderston, the ratio is 20-30 below the national average. It is difficult to relate differences such as these to the effects of affluence.

TABLE IV. Standardised mortality ratios for coronary heart disease
England and Wales (1950)

Social Class	I	II	III	IV	V
S.M.R.	150	110	104	79	89

* The Standard Mortality Ratio is derived by taking the national (in this case United Kingdom) mortality as 100 and relating the local mortality to this figure.

If social class is taken as an index of affluence, however, there seems to be a strongly positive correlation between mortality from coronary heart disease and affluence (Table IV); the S.M.R. is highest in Social Class I (professional classes) and lowest in social classes IV and V (partially skilled and unskilled occupations).[7]

CAUSES OF ISCHAEMIC HEART DISEASE

We do not yet know the cause of coronary artery disease but as a result of intensive epidemiological and other studies during the last decade or so a number of important factors have emerged. Some of these cannot be related to affluence, for example the hereditary factor, the predilection for the male sex and probably the apparent association with the hardness of the water supply. Others, however, do have a close connection with affluence and some of these will now be considered.

Race

The mortality from ischaemic heart disease in different countries has already been considered. That the higher mortality in developed countries is the result of factors associated with life in these countries, and therefore with affluence, is suggested by the observation that the incidence of ischaemic heart disease in immigrant populations is similar to that of the community in which they are living rather than that of their country of origin. This has been shown for several groups, but it is most clearly seen in the U.S.A. where the different ethnic groups, Negroes, Jews, Irish, Chinese, etc. all have a mortality experience from coronary artery disease which is similar to the national average.

Diet

One of the factors which has received a great deal of attention is the dietary one. Most of the work has been concentrated on the fat content of the diet. There are three reasons for this: first, on pathological examination the lesions in the arteries of the heart which are responsible for ischaemic heart disease contain large amounts of fat; secondly, it is known that patients who suffer from ischaemic heart disease frequently have elevated levels of certain lipid (fat) substances, notably cholesterol, in

their blood; and thirdly, it is possible to produce experimentally
in certain animals lesions resembling those of ischaemic heart
disease in man by feeding them a diet containing a lot of
fat.

There is an immense amount of literature on this aspect of
the subject and much has been made of the differences between
animal and vegetable fats, between saturated and poly-
unsaturated fats and of the possible importance of certain
essential fatty acids, notably linolenic acid. It would be impossible to summarise this here and for our present purposes it
is sufficient to make two points:

First it is true to state in general terms that the mean levels
of cholesterol in the blood are higher in populations in advanced, affluent countries than in the inhabitants of underdeveloped, non-affluent countries. Where you have a situation
in which there is a mixed affluent and non-affluent population
as in South Africa a clear correlation can be demonstrated
between income level, the amount of animal fat consumed and
the level of lipids in the blood serum[2] (Table V). There are,
however, some primitive populations, for example the Masai
tribe in East Africa who consume a diet which is rich in animal
fat and yet have low levels of serum lipids and a low mortality

TABLE v. Race, income level, fat consumption and blood lipids

Race	Monthly income £	Animal fat units	Vegetable fat units	Plasma cholesterol mg/100 ml
Bantu	10-35	75-110	10-25	150-200
Cape Coloured	25-50	100-160	40-50	195-225
European	75-200+	160-180	10-35	225-260

from coronary heart disease. Thus in spite of a great deal of
research it is still by no means certain that dietary fat intake is
the important factor responsible for the higher levels of serum
lipids in those who live in an affluent society. Secondly, there is
unequivocal evidence that coronary artery disease is commoner
in individuals with an elevated serum cholesterol. The normal
range of serum cholesterol is 150-250 mg/100 ml with a mean
about 225 mg/100 ml. It has long been accepted that individuals

who have a serum cholesterol level greater than the accepted normal range have a higher incidence of ischaemic heart disease, but what has become apparent from prospective population studies like that carried out at Framingham, Massachusetts is that there is no 'safe' level of cholesterol, that even within the normal range there is a gradation of risk from the lower to the higher levels.[6]

Dietary factors other than fat have also been considered. The suggestion has been made, notably by Professor Yudkin,[15] that it is the amount of sugar (sucrose) rather than the amount of fat in the diet that is responsible for the increase in mortality from ischaemic heart disease. The evidence for this is based on an analysis of the number of cups of tea which patients with arterial disease, including coronary artery disease, consume as compared with a matched group of control subjects. It is to be noted that others have failed to confirm Yudkin's findings.[4] On the other hand, there is evidence that in most developed countries there has been a great increase in the consumption of sugar over the last hundred years or so.[8]

Finally, it is suggested that it is neither fat nor sugar but the total amount of food consumed which is the important dietary factor. There can be no doubt that in an affluent society people consume more kilocalories and at the same time do less in the way of actual physical toil to utilise the excess intake of energy. Many people believe that, if there is a dietary factor responsible for the increased mortality, then it is this combination of what amounts to over-eating and physical sloth which is important rather than any specific dietary change.

Physical activity

One of the features of an affluent society is that fewer people are engaged in honest toil. There is some evidence that the incidence of ischaemic heart disease is related to the amount of regular physical activity which an individual undertakes. A study which is often quoted in this context is that by Professor J. N. Morris[9] in which he showed that London bus drivers had a higher incidence of coronary artery disease than bus conductors. He suggested that one of the explanations for the difference might be that the conductors had a more physically active job collecting fares than the drivers who were sitting for most of their working day. Morris also pointed out, however, that there were other important differences between the two groups; the drivers were on the whole heavier than the conductors and smoked more—but these other possible factors have not attracted the same attention. Similar findings in relation to physical activity have, however, been demonstrated in other occupational groups which are otherwise comparable; post office clerks have a higher incidence of coronary disease than delivery men[5]; the same is true of railway clerks compared with linesmen[11] and farmers in N. Dakota have a lower incidence than sedentary workers in the same state.[16] One of the most interesting studies in this field is that made by Professor Jessop of Dublin and Professor Stare of Harvard.[12] They have made a 'Brother Study' of pairs of Irish and American brothers. The American brother has lived in the U.S.A. for at least 10 years and the Irish brother has remained resident in Ireland. The diet, mode of living, smoking habits and blood pressure of the two brothers has been compared. One of the important differences between the Irish and the American brothers was that more of the former were engaged in occupations involving physical work. Whatever one's personal view about the energy expended by Irish labourers, this certainly lends support to the view that the high incidence of coronary heart disease in the United States may be related to the type of life led by those who live in an affluent society.

Cigarette smoking

The connection between cigarette smoking and lung cancer is now well-established but there is equally good evidence, which is increasing, that there is also a good correlation between the amount of cigarettes which a person smokes and his likelihood of developing and dying from coronary artery disease.[13] This connection can be demonstrated both by the fact that in many countries the death rate from coronary artery disease bears a positive relationship to the monetary expenditure on cigarettes, and in retrospective and prospective studies of populations such as that carried out in Framingham, Massachusetts. Cigarette smoking is not, of course, confined to affluent societies, but the amount smoked and the preference for the more highly refined Virginia tobacco are both factors which are greater in such societies and may well be important in increasing the risk.

Stress

Finally, there is that indefinable condition referred to as 'stress'. It is widely believed that the pressures and pace of life in the twentieth century in an affluent society are important factors in the causation of ischaemic heart disease. The professional men leading a high pressure existence—the business executive, the industrial tycoon, the busy general medical practitioner—these are generally considered to be the people most at risk, and the statistics for mortality related to Social Class already referred to would suggest that this is the case. More recent studies, however, have cast some doubt upon the accuracy of this widely held belief, and anyone who works in an N.H.S. hospital would, I am sure, agree that one sees more patients from the middle income groups with coronary artery disease than from either the top or the bottom ends of the social scale. It is extremely difficult of course to quantify in any way a factor such as stress, but evidence of what happens to the electro-cardiogram of a healthy person when he is driving a car in busy traffic conditions[10] does indicate that at least one stressful situation, which occurs regularly in the daily life of those living in an affluent society, can have a profound effect upon the heart.

CONCLUSION

The effects of affluence upon the heart are, therefore, seen to be a decrease in the incidence and mortality from rheumatic (valvular) heart disease and a dramatic increase in the death rate from arteriosclerotic (ischaemic or coronary) heart disease. While is is easy to explain the improvement in the situation in regard to rheumatic heart disease and to relate this to events that accompany affluence, it is much more difficult to establish a direct connection between affluence and the rising mortality from coronary artery disease. Certain factors such as the nature of the diet, the amount of physical activity, cigarette smoking and, possibly, stress which have different patterns in affluent societies may well play important roles in the causation of this form of heart disease, but the evidence is by no means conclusive. Possibly the development of coronary heart disease is one of the results which stem from the fact to which Professor Garry drew attention in the first chapter that, in an affluent society, man's homeostatic mechanism remains geared to an environment which no longer exists.

REFERENCES

1. Annual reports of the Registrar General for Scotland. H.M.S.O., Edinburgh.
2. Bronte-Stewart, B., 1958. The effect of dietary fats on the blood lipids and their relation to ischaemic heart disease. *Brit. med. Bull.*, **14**, 243.
3. Howe, G. M., 1970. *National atlas of disease mortality in the United Kingdom*, 2nd ed. Nelson, London.
4. Howell, R. W. and Wilson, D. G., 1969. Dietary sugar and ischaemic heart disease. *Brit. med. J.*, **3**, 145.
5. Kahn, H. A., 1963. The relationship of reported coronary heart disease mortality to physical activity of work. *Amer. J. Pub. Health*, **53**, 1058.
6. Kannel, W. B., Dawber, T. R., Friedman, G. D., *et al.*, 1964. Risk factors in coronary heart disease. *Ann. intern. Med.*, **61**, 888.
7. Logan, W. P. D., 1954. Social class variations in mortality. *Public Health Reports*, **69**, 1217.
8. Michaels, L., 1966. Aetiology of coronary heart disease: an historical approach. *Brit. Heart J.*, **28**, 258.
9. Morris, J. N., Kagan, A., Pattison, D. C., *et al.*, 1966. Incidence and prediction of ischaemic heart disease in London busmen. *Lancet*, **2**, 553.
10. Taggart, P., Gibbons, D. and Somerville, W., 1969. Some effects of motor-car driving on the normal and abnormal heart. *Brit. med. J.*, **4**, 130.
11. Taylor, H. L., Klepetar, E., Keys, A., *et al.*, 1962. Death rates among physically active and sedentary employees of the railroad industry. *Amer. J. Pub. Health*, **52**, 169.
12. Trulson, M. F., Clancy, R. E., Jessop, W. J., *et al.*, 1964. Comparison of siblings in Boston and Ireland. *J. Amer. Diet. Ass.*, **45**, 225.
13. U.S. Department Health, Education and Welfare, 1967. The health consequences of smoking. *Public health services review*, Washington.
14. World Health Organisation, 1969. *World health statistics report*, **22**, 448.
15. Yudkin, J. and Roddy, J., 1964. Levels of dietary sucrose in patients with occlusive atherosclerotic disease. *Lancet*, **2**, 6.
16. Zukel, W. J., Lewis, R. H., Enterkine, P. E., *et al.*, 1959. A short-term community study of the epidemiology of heart disease. *Amer. J. Pub. Health*, **49**, 1630.

R. E. WALLER

Affluence and the air

Air pollution comes mainly from the combustion of fuel to serve man's needs for warmth and power. These needs have increased through the centuries, and when they are met by the careless use of fuel they lead to increasing amounts of pollution. However, in many areas a turning point has already been reached. Given sufficient incentive, including ample financial resources, it is possible to produce heat and power efficiently and conveniently without creating serious pollution problems.

In Britain, wood and charcoal at one time served all the needs for heat and crude industrial processes, but gradually, from the end of the thirteenth century, coal began to take over. Originally, it was known as 'sea-coal', being carried by sea from Newcastle; by the seventeenth century it was the main fuel for industrial purposes, and it was reluctantly accepted by 'polite society' in London for domestic heating, as wood became scarce. The smoke and fumes from coal had always been regarded as far more unpleasant than those from wood, and the situation in London was already bad enough in 1661 for Evelyn, the famous diarist, to present a discourse to Charles II, which he entitled *Fumifugium*.[2] He had no doubt about the cause of the nuisance, saying that 'the immoderate use of, and indulgence to Sea-Coale alone in the City of London, exposes it to one of the fowlest Inconveniences and reproaches, than possibly befall so noble, and otherwise incomparable City'. Evelyn commented on the damage to buildings, ironwork, furniture, paintings and clothes, and reported at length on the ill-effects on health. In this he was criticised by the College of Physicians, who considered the smoke to be a preservation against infections.

Despite Evelyn's words, and those of many others, there was a relentless increase in pollution by coal smoke during the period of the industrial revolution. Smoke was a sign of 'brass',

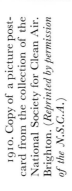

1910. Copy of a picture post-
card from the collection of the
National Society for Clean Air.
Brighton. (*Reprinted by permission
of the N.S.C.A.*)

1969. Copy of similar view
taken by the British Ceramic
Research Association, Stoke on
Trent. (*Reprinted by permission of
the B.C.R.A.*)

Electron micrograph of smoke aggregates and other particles in sample collected amidst heavy traffic. (*Reprinted by permission of the M.R.C. Air Pollution Unit.*)

and the wealth of an area was judged by the number of chimneys belching forth black smoke. It was not just the smoke from industrial chimneys that made life so unpleasant in the towns of this country during the nineteenth century, it was the smoke from the thousands of domestic chimneys serving coal fires in virtually every house. In London then it might well have been true to say that there was a direct link between affluence and pollution: in the large houses of the well-to-do, servants stoked fires for cooking, and carried coal around the house to living rooms and bedrooms alike.

This era was brought to a close by the First World War, which so altered social activities that the carrying of coal to diverse fires in large houses became out of the question. This is when affluence began to have its beneficial effects on pollution —those with sufficient money were able to turn to the more efficient use of solid fuels in central heating plants, or to 'cleaner' fuels, such as gas, electricity, and later, oil. Industry, too, began to put its house in order, as technical improvements and increased capital investment led to the more efficient use of fuel. Tradition, however, dies hard, and old-fashioned methods of heating and power generation were retained at least into the 1950's, when the disastrous fog in London (December, 1952) finally led the government to take action on a national scale.[6]

Whatever steps are taken to reduce the emission of pollution, one must always guard against the rare meteorological condition—i.e. a temperature inversion at a few hundred feet—that holds in all the pollution emitted under it. That is the great problem in Los Angeles, where by our standards the emissions of traditional pollutants into the air are trivial, but since their otherwise enviable climate leads to frequent temperature inversions, anything that is emitted stays there for long periods. The 'smog' for which they are notorious comes from complex photo-chemical reactions between constituents of exhausts from the millions of cars that are in use there.[3] Affluence has indeed led the inhabitants of that city into difficulties, and the cure must lie in spending more money on control devices, or in the development of alternative transportation systems.

Despite the outstanding reduction in smoke emission in recent years, there are still major problems of pollution in the cities of this country. Pollution by sulphur compounds continues, and in these changing conditions we need to know more not only about the gross amounts of pollution, but also about the character of the pollutants. Microscopic studies show that not all the particles in the air are black sooty ones: crystalline substances (notably ammonium sulphate) and acid droplets are present too.[10] The black particles themselves are extremely small, and to examine them individually it is necessary to use the electron microscope.[12] Examples of the size and number of suspended particles in London air are given in Table I.[4] These tiny particles are the ones responsible for dirtying clothes, buildings and other surfaces, and they are certainly small enough to pass through the upper respiratory tract and reach the lungs.

TABLE I. Number and size of particles in London air

Sampling site	No. of particles/ml	No. Median diameter (μm)	Estimated concentration ($\mu g/m^3$)	Mass median diameter (μm)
City, normal pollution	7,800	0·09	100	0·7
City, moderate pollution	27,100	0·09	370	0·8
City, high pollution	154,500	0·10	1,970	0·9
Street sample, light traffic	27,300	0·12	280	0·5
Tunnel sample, heavy traffic	120,400	0·09	1,260	0·7

The net result of present policies for smoke control has been to bring smoke concentrations in many large towns down to, or even below, those in small towns.[15] The highest smoke concentrations are to be found among the rows of terraced houses in the 'twilight' areas of industrial towns, or even in some villages. One powerful force in the elimination of the coal fire is the advent of television. The 'flickering flames' were at one time the focus of attention in a room, but now the 'flickering screen' is taking over, and in some areas chimneys are more useful for holding up television aerials than for dispersing pollution.

The effects of pollution on health have at no time been more obvious than in the 1952 fog episode in London, in which 4,000 people died.[6] The death-toll in the last episode of that type, in 1962, was much smaller, but it was still outstanding. Figure 1

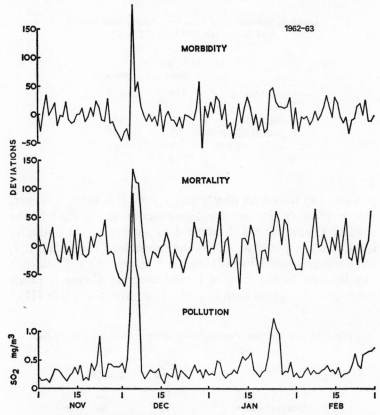

Figure 1. Daily changes in mortality and in morbidity (requests for admission to hospital), Greater London, winter 1962-63. The figures relate to deviations from 15-day moving averages.

shows that there was a sudden increase in deaths and in the demand for hospital beds at that time, coinciding with the increase in pollution.[14]

The long-term effects of exposure to pollution are difficult to isolate, but they are no less important. Some of the smoke inhaled is retained in the lungs; it is common for the lungs of town-dwellers to be blackened by smoke, and some may have all the tissue destroyed. Pollution is not the only factor contributing to this massive deterioration: smoking habits are im-

TABLE II. Standardised mortality ratios, lung cancer
and bronchitis, 1961-65 (M & F)

	Lung cancer	Bronchitis
Conurbations	119	116
Urban—		
100,000+	107	115
50-100,000	97	95
under 50,000	87	92
Rural	79	74

portant, and infections play a major part. It is clear, however, that respiratory diseases are commoner in towns than in the country (Table II).[9] This alone does not prove that pollution is the factor responsible, and in the case of lung cancer it is not, but it suggests useful lines of enquiry. A reverse effect of affluence can be seen in the case of bronchitis: this disease is much commoner in manual than in professional workers (Table III).[8]

TABLE III. Standardised mortality ratio by social class (M, 20-64)

	Lung cancer	Bronchitis
1. professional	80	33
2. intermediate	79	53
3. skilled	108	97
4. partly skilled	89	103
5. unskilled	116	172

The difference in lung cancer mortality between areas with differing amounts of pollution, interesting as it may be, is small compared with that between smokers and non-smokers, and there is no doubt that in this disease cigarette smoking is of overwhelming importance (Table IV).[1, 11]
    One field in which affluence is of direct relevance is pollution

from motor vehicles. Whilst their total contribution to pollution is small in comparison with that from domestic and industrial sources, they are of special interest, since everything is discharged

TABLE IV. Lung cancer death rates per 100,000

Gen. popn.	Salford	295
M, 45-64	Eastbourne	194
1958-64	Rural Districts	132
Doctors	25+ cigs./day	227
M, 35+	15-24 cigs./day	139
1951-61	1-14 cigs./day	57
	non-smokers	7

close to breathing level, and they provide the main source of one particular pollutant, carbon monoxide. In one interesting series of experiments that we did some years ago, we made measurements in the middle of Fleet Street to examine the extent of pollution by motor vehicles.[13] The results for carbon monoxide reflected the pattern of traffic there (Fig. 2). Whilst brief peaks occurred up to 100 p.p.m. and more, the average concentration (17 p.p.m. during daytime hours) was not alarming, and it was of relevance only to those people who spent a large part of their working day there. These included, at the time, policemen on point duty, but blood samples taken from men as they came off duty only succeeded in discriminating between smokers and non-smokers. Carbon monoxide is present in cigarette smoke as well as in exhausts from petrol engines, and our results showed that the amount that can be taken up through smoking cigarettes is in general larger than that acquired from street air.

Development of a simple and relatively non-traumatic way of taking and examining blood samples has enabled us to do much more work of this type, and the results have shown so far that even for people occupationally exposed to carbon monoxide in garages, customs sheds. and the holds of ferry boats, smoking is usually a more important factor than the environment.[5] When we shut subjects away in a chamber and asked them to chainsmoke cigarettes, we found that it was possible for them to reach high, though still not alarming, levels of carbon

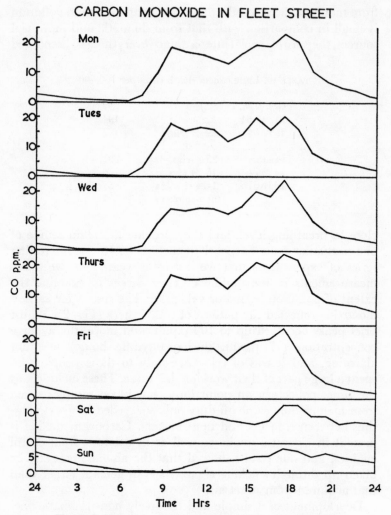

Figure 2. Hourly mean concentrations of carbon monoxide in Fleet Street.

monoxide in their blood. Blood levels below 10% saturation do not, according to the literature, produce any obvious symptoms, and we have not, in normal smoking or street exposures observed anything in excess of that figure. We are, however, currently considering the effects of low levels of carbon monoxide in the blood, following experimental inhalations. Tests devised by applied psychologists have been used to see if the performance of fine tasks is affected in any way. The practical interest in this work is the possibility that driving ability might be affected by carbon monoxide when travelling in dense traffic for long periods. The Paris police have expressed great interest in this in relation to accidents in urban areas,[7] and although it has led them to propose several measures for reducing carbon monoxide concentrations in busy streets, there is no positive evidence that such effects occur.

In this necessarily brief review it has only been possible to touch on some aspects of current research in the field of air pollution, but it is perhaps clear that affluence is a mixed blessing as far as pollution is concerned. It is also clear that investigations into effects on health can be very complicated, requiring co-operation between clinicians, chemists, physicists, physiologists, biologists, psychologists, engineers and statisticians. There are in fact few areas of research where interdisciplinary studies are more essential.

REFERENCES

1. Doll, R. and Hill, A. B., 1964. Mortality in relation to smoking: ten years' observation of British doctors. *Brit. med. J.*, 1, 1399.
2. Evelyn, J., 1661. *Fumifugium*. 1961, reprinted by National Society for Clean Air, London.
3. Goldsmith, J. R., 1969. Los Angeles smog. *Science Journal*, 5, 44.
4. Lawther, P. J., Ellison, J. McK. and Waller, R. E., 1968. Some medical aspects of aerosol research. *Proc. Roy. Soc. Ser. A.*, 307, 223.
5. Lawther, P. J. and Commins, B. T., 1970. Cigarette smoking and exposure to CO. In: *Conf. on Biological effects of Carbon monoxide, New York*. Academy of Sciences, New York.
6. Ministry of Health, 1954. Mortality and morbidity during the London fog of December 1952. *Rep. on Pub. Hlth. and Medical Subjects*, No. 95. H.M.S.O., London.
7. Préfecture de Police. Études de pollution atmosphérique à Paris et dans les Départements périphériques. *Annual reports published by Laboratoire Central*, Paris.
8. Registrar General, 1957. *Decennial supplement. England and Wales 1951, Occupational mortality, Part II*. H.M.S.O., London.
9. Registrar General, 1968, *Statistical review of England and Wales for 1965, Part 3, Commentary*. H.M.S.O., London.
10. Waller, R. E., 1963. Acid droplets in town air. *Int. J. Air Water Poll.*, 7, 773.

11. Waller, R. E., 1967. Smoke, smoking and lung cancer. *Trans. Int. Chest and Heart Conf.*, Eastbourne, p. 155. Chest and Heart Association, London.
12. Waller, R. E., Brooks, A. G. F. and Cartwright, J., 1963. An electron microscope study of particles in town air. *Int. J. Air Water Poll.*, **7**, 779.
13. Waller, R. E., Commins, B. T. and Lawther, P. J., 1965. Air pollution in a city street. *Brit. J. industr. Med.*, **22**, 128.
14. Waller, R. E., Lawther, P. J. and Martin, A. E., 1969. Clean air and health in London. *Proc. Eastbourne Conf.*, p. 71. National Society for Clean Air, London.
15. Warren Spring Laboratory, 1971. *National survey of air pollution, Report No. 1.* H.M.S.O., London.

FURTHER READING

Air pollution. 3 vols. A. C. Stern (ed.). 2nd edition. Academic Press, New York. 1968.

Air pollution abstracts. Distributed monthly to local authorities and others engaged in measurement. Warren Spring Laboratory, Stevenage.

Air pollution and health. Report for the Royal College of Physicians. Pitman, London. 1970.

Atmospheric environment. A monthly journal published by Pergamon Press, Oxford.

Clean Air year book. Published annually by National Society for Clean Air, Brighton.

The investigation of air pollution. 32nd Report. H.M.S.O., London. 1967.

J. IAN WADDINGTON

Affluence and water

Man existed on this earth for thousands of years without
causing significant water pollution and, by and large, other
forms of life do not cause it either, unless the natural regime has
become distorted by *Homo sapiens*. The growth of water pollution as a general problem has followed the expansion of the
human population and the development of larger urban communities, industry and intensive agriculture. Paradoxically, the
control of waterborne diseases by the provision of safe public
supplies has been one of the factors leading to the present
population explosion and this in turn is aggravating the water
pollution problem.

Clearly, the most fundamental danger to man of polluted
water is the threat to his drinking water by contamination of
either an existing supply or of a potential source, thereby
restricting the amount available. In addition to health hazards,
pollution may affect the economy by rendering water unusable
by industry and it may even cause corrosion damage to struc-
tures and equipment on land or at sea. It can affect his food
supply, both by damaging fisheries and by contaminating water
used for livestock or irrigation. It can prejudice his enjoyment
of life by marring the beauty of lake and stream and by limiting
his use of open waters for bathing, boating, swimming or fishing.
Finally, it can cause damage to wildlife, increasingly regarded
as an important part of man's heritage.

Availability of an adequate supply of clean and wholesome
drinking water is a basic requirement of civilised society. The
development of an understanding of bacterial infection and
sterilisation techniques has led to the rapid decline of former
serious waterborne diseases, although much yet remains to be
accomplished in the less advanced countries, particularly in
Africa and Asia.

One hundred and fifty years ago in Britain, many virtually

untreated supplies were drawn from rivers and it was another public health development which ironically led to an increase in waterborne disease, namely the widespread adoption of the water carriage system of sewage disposal. Previously, wastes were usually collected within or near dwellings and removed manually. This was a laborious, unhealthy and unpleasant procedure but it did not in itself lead to much water pollution. With more general adoption of sewerage systems, many rivers became incredibly filthy and there was a reaction against the concept of water carriage of wastes. In Glasgow, the cry went up 'rainfall to rivers and sewage to the soil'.

During the nineteenth century increasing efforts were made to develop a satisfactory system of sewage purification. Much of the work was carried out by private enterprise and was largely motivated by the apparent prospect of fortunes to be made by the economic recovery of by-products, such as the evaporation of sewage to produce ammonia. It was only when sewage purification became regarded as an essential public health service that real progress began to be achieved. Since the beginning of the present century, techniques have developed to the point where it is practicable, but seldom economic, to produce potable water from sewage. Logically, the process of purification is taken to the point where the receiving water-course can deal satisfactorily with any remaining impurity.

During the first industrial revolution, many manufacturing processes were developed which caused water pollution, including those at paper mills, textile plants and gas works. Since that time the quantity of trade effluents produced has increased greatly and they are more diverse and more complex. If these wastes were all discharged untreated, rivers in industrialised areas would be polluted to the extent that many factories would have to close down because their own supplies would be too contaminated—industry would then be truly 'fouling its own nest'. But it is significant that, although industry, including agriculture, has such a vital interest in clean water, much of the pressure for improvements has resulted from public demands for an improved environment.

As with sewage purification, there is now a complex technology devoted to trade effluent treatment and most industrial wastes can be purified satisfactorily, either in admixture with sewage (perhaps after pre-treatment before discharge to the sewer) or by the installation of a complete treatment process at the factory. There is an increasing tendency for closed-cycle water usage systems to be installed, sometimes almost eliminating the necessity to discharge effluents and leading to great economies in the nett quantity of water required. Sometimes, but not always, firms have the incentive of recovering useful by-products such as the processing of distillery wastes to produce cattle-feed and the treatment of plating shop effluents to recover metals.

Many countries have now introduced legislation to control the discharge of polluting matter to streams, lakes and the sea. In Britain in 1876 the responsibility for controlling pollution was vested in local authorities but, as they themselves were the major offenders, the system was not very satisfactory. In 1951, river boards were entrusted with the task. This has proved to be a sound policy, as, in spite of rapidly increasing demands for water and a growing complexity in the nature of wastes discharged, few British rivers have deteriorated since that time. Many improvements have been achieved, even though public expenditure on treatment plants has been limited by recurrent national restrictions on capital expenditure.

Higher standards of effluent purity are now being required as water demands increase. The water in some rivers is already being used several times [4, 10] (see Table I).

TABLE I. Usage of river water in the Clyde valley, Scotland (1969)

River	Volume of sewage and trade effluent (m^3/day)	Low river flow (m^3/day)	'Used' water (per cent of low river flow)	Drought river flow (m^3/day)	'Used' water (per cent of drought river flow)
Clyde (non-tidal)	482,112 (1,849,824)*	915,840	53(202)*	596,160	81(310)*
Kelvin	45,792	129,600	35	70,848	65
North Calder	54,432	60,480	90	31,104	175
South Calder	40,608	79,488	51	67,392	60
Rotten Calder	4,320	9,504	45	6,048	71
White Cart	104,544	95,040	110	66,528	157
Black Cart	13,824	67,392	21	31,968	43

* Including power station usage.

The growth rate of a country's economy is accompanied by a roughly equivalent increase in water consumption (see Table II).

TABLE II. Public water supply: estimated demands in the North of England[11]

Year	Consumption per head (litres per day)	Total consumption (m³/d)	Industrial consumption (m³/d)
1967	278	4,160,000	1,820,000
1981	—	6,255,000	3,000,000
2001	455	8,740,000	4,270,000

If pollution is to be controlled there must be a corresponding investment in purification plant. Expenditure on sewage purification has long been regarded as a valid and appropriate charge on rates or taxes: that on trade effluent treatment is now being accepted as an integral part of production costs.

Man needs water free from harmful or unpleasant chemical contaminants and from those bacteria, protozoa and arthropods which might cause disease. Risk of disease from drinking water has greatly diminished due to greater understanding of the medical factors involved and development of the appropriate technology. But growing demands have led to the increasing use of river sources which have been exposed to substantial pollution. Many of the contaminants are either difficult to remove or are present in very minute concentrations, sometimes at the extreme limit of present methods of detection. They may sometimes be concentrated through food chains and reach man as part of his food. Sewage bacteria, for example, are readily concentrated by filter-feeding mussels, *Mytilus edulis*, and may cause food-poisoning where mussels have been collected from a bed exposed to sewage and inadequately prepared.

The variety of contaminants has led to increasing awareness of the risks of possible somatic or genetic effects, perhaps only after the particular source has been ingested over long periods (see chapter on the genetic effects of contaminants).

Just after the Second World War, the introduction of synthetic detergents (Table III), a large proportion of which were

(*Above*) A product of affluence: unauthorised dumping of garbage.
(*Below*) A small stream of which half the flow is sewage effluent.

(*Reprinted by permission of Rupert Roddam.*)

branched-chain alkyl aryl sulphonates and largely resistant to biological degradation in treatment plants and rivers, became a cause for concern in drinking waters.

TABLE III. U.K. consumption of anionic detergents and soap products (thousands of tons)[7]

	Anionic surface active material	Soap products (as sold)
1949	13·0	497
1950	15·2	575
1951	17·6	505
1952	26·2	440
1953	35·0	418
1954	39·0	400
1955	40·5	410
1956	41·0	410
1957	41·0	418
1958	41·3	386
1959	44·9	388
1960	48·7	391
1961	51·2	384
1962	51·5	377
1963	52	367
1964	56	367
1965	59	326
1966	60	321
1967	64	299
1968	69	290
1969	72	250

Also, the foam which appeared on many rivers and at treatment plants, possibly containing pathogenic bacteria and eggs of parasitic worms, could be carried quite large distances by wind. 'Soft' detergents have now been developed which are more easily amenable to biological decomposition.

At coke-oven plants and in other industrial processes, phenols are produced which, unless removed by adequate treatment before discharge, can cause unpleasant taste in water supplies drawn further downstream. If the water is chlorinated, chlorophenols are produced which cause detectable taste in concentrations as low as 0·001 mg/l. This problem is at present being experienced by the City of Budapest water undertaking, which supplies two million consumers, largely from waters drawn directly from the River Danube: in this case the phenols arise from industrial discharges in countries further upstream. Chlorophenols and traces of other organic materials also affect Dutch water supplies drawn from the River Rhine after its passage through the Ruhr and other industrial areas.

Nitrates are produced by the breakdown and subsequent oxidation of protein nitrogen in sewage and their presence has often been regarded as a criterion of a satisfactory effluent. However, if they are present in concentrations greater than 10-20 mg/l in water supplies, they can cause methaemoglobinaemia in young babies.

In general, industrialisation and resulting affluence is followed by the virtual elimination of waterborne disease. But health, as defined by the World Health Organisation, includes 'well-being', which implies a satisfactory environment. Even though industrialisation is usually accompanied by the provision of a satisfactory public water supply, the majority of streams passing through urban areas are now polluted to a greater or lesser extent and this may not only interfere with the exploitation of the water to meet man's material needs but may interfere with his enjoyment of his surroundings.

Although pollution can affect all species of flora and fauna, its aesthetic impact is perhaps only experienced by man. Whereas affluence has increased the problem of water pollution due to the greater production of domestic water-borne wastes from garbage grinders, washing machines and showers, etc. and of industrial wastes from the ever widening range of goods available to and being demanded by society, it is also leading to shorter working hours and the money necessary to create a wider choice of leisure pursuits. The pressures inherent in a modern industrial society have led to an increasing desire to get away into rural surroundings. Many outdoor leisure pursuits depend on the availability of water—swimming, yachting, rowing, water skiing, fishing, bird watching and even the contemplation of landscape: a high proportion of beauty spots depend on water for much of their appeal. The ambition of many city dwellers in Europe and America is now a weekend retreat in the country or at the coast. Linear parks following the line of rivers, such as the Lee Valley scheme near London, are being planned. All such leisure use of water demands an adequate control of pollution. Thus, affluence can provide challenging opportunities, but if the benefits are taken irresponsibly, the challenge can become a mockery.

Recreational use of water can itself create pollution problems, for example the discharge of sewage and oil from pleasure boats and the careless disposal of the contents of chemical closets at camp sites. International air travel by jet plane has led to added risks of introducing new water-borne diseases. A party of businessmen can be shooting over moorland within a water supply catchment only a few hours after arriving from another country or even another continent. Although modern methods of water purification minimise the health risk, as they depend not merely on one effective stage of treatment but on several lines of defence, viral diseases can occur and the incidence of infective hepatitis has recently been investigated.[5]

Although streams and coastal waters may be biologically and chemically satisfactory, their aesthetic appeal may be marred by the presence of garbage. Natural deposits of vegetable material are eventually broken down by bacterial decay, as are cans and waste paper, whilst broken glass is eventually ground to powder by the action of the sea. But post-war affluence has led to an explosive expansion of the packaging industry, using non-degradable plastics which persist in the environment almost unchanged. These detract from the appearance of beaches and river banks and can also cause damage, as for example polythene sheeting wrapping around the propeller shafts of vessels.

A further problem is the creation of dereliction by the abandonment of sites used for temporary or obsolete industrial activity. This can cause serious water pollution, particularly where chemicals have been deposited.

Movement of goods by road, rail and ship can also result in serious water pollution following accidents. There is a pressing need for accurate labelling of toxic chemicals and, in many cases, drivers of vehicles are unaware of the nature of their loads. Many products are under a brand name and they may be compiled by a marketing firm from chemicals manufactured by several different companies. It is therefore extremely difficult to assess the threat of pollution in cases of emergency.

Perhaps there is no more direct measure of affluence today

than the extent of car ownership: in Europe, this has certainly
not yet reached saturation. The refining of crude oil to produce
petroleum and other products has greatly expanded during the
last few years (Table IV): oil tankers now dominate the sea-
lanes of the world. Not surprisingly, contamination by oil has

TABLE IV. Oil refining capacity, million metric tons[3]

	France	Germany	Italy	U.K.	Netherlands
1938	7·6	2·4	2·1	1·9	0·8
1950	15·7	4·7	5·6	11·5	5·6
1960	40·4	39·7	41·4	49·3	23·0
1968	93·4	112·0	144·0	97·0	42·0

attracted more attention from the population in general than
any other form of pollution: even thin films are visible and
bodily contact with oil in water or on a beach is immediately
and unpleasantly obvious. Pollution can occur during the refining of oil, but most arises during its transport, distribution,
and disposal after use. Whilst the major oil companies have
displayed great concern over the extent of pollution, the formu-
lation of international agreements to govern the transportation
of oil by sea is a long and complex process; there is no effective
means of securing their adoption by all maritime nations, as
the high seas continue to be regarded as being beyond the
jurisdiction of any country or group of countries.

A new proposal to limit the discharge of dirty ballast water
from tankers to distances more than 50 miles from the shore and
then a maximum of 60 litres per mile of ships' travel, was introduced in 1969 by the Intergovernmental Maritime Consultative Organisation, an agency of the United Nations. So far
only Britain and the United States are taking steps to adopt
this system, which is certainly a great advance on previous
proposals. The international problem of oil pollution admirably
demonstrates the need for multilateral co-operation in order to
secure satisfactory management of the environment, including
the oceans. Thor Heyerdahl, describing his recent voyage across
the Atlantic by raft, reported that he had not encountered any
area of ocean which was free from oil.

Eventually off-shore drilling may lead to less oil being

shipped across the world, but the drilling itself can cause pollution. At Santa Barbara on the coast of California, oil leaking from the vicinity of an off-shore well has proved extremely difficult to contain.

There has always been an obvious advantage in returning organic wastes to the land and, in many places, sewage sludge has been used as a fertiliser, sometimes after anaerobic digestion. Difficulties have increased over recent years due to the extent and variety of harmful constituents in the sludge. The digestion process itself can be adversely affected by as little as 1 mg/l.[1] of pentachlorophenol. Chromium, nickel and many other metals which may be present in sludges may inhibit soil bacteria.

The effect of detergents on water supplies has already been discussed. Many of these materials contain phosphate 'builders' which have increased the enrichment process due to the discharge of fertilising salts to lakes and rivers. Excessive algal blooms have occurred in many waters during the last few years, including Lake Erie. Photosynthesis of such blooms causes a marked diurnal variation in the dissolved oxygen content of the water, with the critical minimum value being reached during the hours of darkness and a corresponding fluctuation in pH, with levels as high as 10·5 being reached during the day.[9] Such growths have an impact on man by fouling sources of drinking water,[6] damaging fisheries and causing unsightly, unpleasant conditions along bathing beaches, particularly during periods when the bloom is decomposing.

Boron is also present in many detergents and when discharged to a stream it can affect certain crops if the water is used for their irrigation.[7]

The last few years have seen increasing concern about the effect of pesticides on wildlife, particularly in America. D.D.T. has been extremely successful in controlling harmful insects and giving large sections of the earth's population their first real chance to come to terms with their environment and achieve a reasonable standard of living. But its continued use, and that of even more toxic and resistant compounds, has led to disquiet about their long-term effects. D.D.T. has become distributed in organic material throughout the world and substantial concentrations have been recorded in human tissue.

An example of the biological chain responsible for the concentration of insecticides has occurred in the Glasgow area where, in addition to general use by the community, they are used for moth proofing by carpet manufacturers. Minute traces pass to the sewers and hence into the Clyde estuary, where in 1967 they accumulated in mussels *Mytilus edulis* to the extent of 0·099 mg/l dieldrin and 0·089 mg/l D.D.T.

By similar concentration processes, organic mercury compounds discharged from chemical works in Japan have been responsible for the so-called Minamata disease which has killed and paralysed people eating fish in the area of the discharges.[2]

The need is now realised for comprehensive investigation into the effects of new chemicals on man, on organisms in biological treatment plants and in the environment generally. Increasingly, sporadic snap sampling for chemical analysis of river and marine waters is being augmented by continuous monitoring of certain parameters, although the equipment available is not yet thoroughly satisfactory. Biological monitoring of bottom fauna is becoming recognised as an essential part of river basin management, often using a system of biotic indices[8, 9] based on the 'spectrum' of organisms present. Such work is laborious and difficult to interpret, but it is capable of achieving important results. Chemical analysis alone can not be expected to cover all possible harmful constituents and sporadic sampling can miss waves of pollution, perhaps occurring at night.

It is clear that there is going to be a need for more comprehensive sampling and examination of fish, birds and other life in order to monitor changes in concentration of particular substances and groups of substances.

As the quantity and diversity of wastes and the resulting cost to the community increases, there must be further economic studies of water pollution. It is well known that the presence of trade effluents can add greatly to the expense of sewage purification; in many cases some or all of the cost is recovered from the industry. The real cost of detergents to the housewife should include the cost of the extra plant needed to purify domestic sewage since their introduction. The cost of oil to the consumer might include a levy to subsidise a service for the collection of waste oil after use.

Increased affluence implies increased water usage and therefore more pollution, unless funds are made available to ensure that the answers to the technical problems are known in good time and the necessary investment made in purification plant. Unless water pollution control facilities are regarded as public utilities in the same way as gas, electricity and water, to be provided in advance or at the same time as development rather than years later, rivers and marine waters will deteriorate.

It is only now that we are beginning to measure the cost of stress due to overcrowding, pollution and the lack of provision for leisure pursuits. But the development of water resources can, if carried out wisely, provide new facilities for recreation and new habitats for wildlife. Limitations on suitable sources of supply are encouraging the adoption of multi-purpose concepts where integrated resource management can allow the compatible use of water for public supply, agriculture, industry, fisheries and for amenity purposes.

Whereas it may be possible to assess the value of fishing and boating, the visual appeal of unsullied water is much more difficult to measure and the influence of pollution on human well-being is particularly hard to quantify in terms which will satisfy an economist. But familiarity with economic concepts is a discipline which environmental biologists will have to master.

There are grounds for cautious optimism. The technology of most aspects of water treatment and reclamation is already known. If adequate funds are available for the conservation of water resources and for the provision of treatment plants, if monitoring is carried out to ensure that dangerous concentration effects of organic materials are avoided and if there is thorough surveillance of materials which could cause new water pollution problems, then there is no reason to suppose that affluence need prejudice the satisfaction of man's physical, economic and psychological needs for clean water.

REFERENCES

1. Drew, E. A. and Swanwick, J. D., 1962. Sludge treatment at Rye Meads: consequences of a recent inhibition of digestion. *J.D. Inst. P.H.E.*, **61**, 216.

2. Irukayama, K., 1966. The pollution of Minamata Bay and Minamata Disease. *Water Pollution Research*, 3rd. International Conf., Munich.
3. Jagger, H., 1970. The growth of petroleum production and movement. *Water pollution by oil*, I.W.P.C./W.H.O. Seminar, Aviemore, Scotland.
4. Lester, W. F., 1967. River water quality management in the Trent River Authority area. *J. Inst. W.P.C.*, 4, 321.
5. Morley, J. W., 1963. Epidemiological aspects of viral agents in relation to waterborne disease. *Pub. Health Report*, 78, 328.
6. Owens, M. and Wood, G., 1968. Some aspects of the eutrophication of water. *Water Research*, 2, 151.
7. Standing Committee on Synthetic Detergents, 1970-71. *11th and 12th progress reports*, H.M.S.O., London.
8. *Trent River Board*, 1957-61. 2nd quinquennial abstract of statistics, p. 91.
9. Waddington, J. I., 1957. *Cladophora* development in the River Tweed. *J. Inst. S.P.*, 2, 178.
10. Waddington, J. I., 1968. A matter of priorities. *River pollution prevention*, I.W.P.C. Symposium, Edinburgh, p. 20.
11. Water Resources Board, 1970. *Water resources in the north*. H.M.S.O., London.

Food additives and contaminants

If affluence is reflected at its peak in the United States of America, it is symptomatic that that country has the most comprehensive system of food legislation to be found anywhere. Its major feature is the control of food additives and contaminants and it is pertinent that the reader of this book should reflect on this kind of legislation. What purposes does it seek to serve and how effectively can these purposes be defined and implemented? Before we can begin to examine this we must try to clarify three simple questions. What is a food? What is an additive? What is a contaminant?

The word 'food' implies different things to different people. In common usage it conveys a mental image of farm and kitchen and the assumption that the natural products of the land which we are accustomed to consider as foods are health-giving, wholesome, nutritious and free from objectionable substances. Yet, should anyone subscribe to such a view, I commend to him or her a publication of the United States National Academy of Sciences entitled *Toxicants occurring naturally in foods*.[6] It runs to 284 pages, and after reading it one is drawn to the conclusion that, whatever kind of diet one favours, a determination to avoid all toxic substances in food will lead to an early death through starvation. This is admirably illustrated by Dr Magnus Pyke in his recently published book *Food and society*.[8] After pointing out that when a new food or food additive is proposed in a modern industrialised community, it must first be subjected to prolonged toxicological testing before official approval is obtained, he adds (and I quote):

> 'The tests are in fact so stringent that if Sir Walter Raleigh turned up now with the potato, as a new and unknown food, he would never stand a chance of having it accepted. Potatoes contain a poisonous substance, solanine. Wholesome potato tubers contain about 90 parts of

solanine per million. This concentration may fairly readily increase if, for example, dug potatoes are exposed for long to the sun. Potatoes containing 400 parts per million have been associated with outbreaks of poisoning. It is a remarkable social paradox that educated nations accept quite calmly the daily use of a foodstuff commonly containing a toxic agent, of which five times more would prove harmful. It is usual to insist on a hundred-fold margin of safety for anything new.'

Having found that the natural foods, which we have hitherto assumed wholesome, actually contain a quite remarkable array of toxic substances, we must conclude from the survival of *Homo sapiens* that our bodies are well able to cope with these provided that they are not expected to deal with too much at any one time.

When we next begin to consider the nature of food additives, the term itself raises the question 'when is a food not a food?' To a chemist synthetic ascorbic acid is simply another chemical despite the fact that it is identical with the vitamin C found in fruit and vegetables. To certain members of the general public ascorbic acid is a chemical additive and vitamin C is a food. To the specialist this is a mere quibble; but when we consider that the prospect of synthetic food, which a mere three or four years ago I would have regarded as a remote future prospect, is gradually becoming a practical possibility, the quibble becomes less academic. From trends which have been more noticeable in scientific reports from a range of recent sources, I now expect to eat and enjoy purely synthetic foods should I survive my allotted span. The definitive experiments have already been carried out, and extensive tests have shown that young male volunteers improved in health after six months on a purely synthetic diet.[9] For general use, the cost of such a diet is prohibitive at the moment. However, this kind of work, begun by the American Space Agency, will doubtless continue there and in other centres. It will be developed first for such special purposes and for clinical application, for example, in the treatment of cystic fibrosis, but I am confident (for reasons which the confines of this chapter do not allow me to explore) that synthetic food is an economic possibility for the future, and perhaps the comparatively near future at that.

Thus we move from a mental picture of the farm-fresh food of our youth, through an intermediate stage represented by the present in which there is a certain public unease that food is being devalued by the addition of chemicals, to a not too distant future in which a purely synthetic diet, that is to say a purely chemical diet, may not be merely a scientific novelty, but an economic necessity by sheer pressure of population expansion. So much has been said and written about this expansion that the imagination is blunted by astronomical figures. Perhaps it will be sharpened if I put the issue in this form: the world's population has increased as much in my lifetime as it did between the birth of Christ and the year 1920. This is a fact which we must keep clearly before us when we speak of the Biology of Affluence.

Our third difficulty lies in defining a contaminant. If your waiter leaves a greasy thumb-print on your plate, or you find a tiny worm in your fresh salad, you rightly object. Yet neither worm nor thumb-print as such will do you much harm. At the same time the thought of food contamination is repellent and is associated in our minds with emotive ideas such as food poisoning or filth. Yet food contamination may be life-saving. Take the case of the vegan, the strict vegetarian, who will not consume food of animal origin. But vitamin B_{12} is an essential nutrient and vitamin B_{12} is absent from a vegetable diet. Yet veganism has been practised in some parts of the world for centuries and its devotees have often appeared perfectly healthy. On the other hand, strict veganism in Britain is a form of slow but certain suicide unless the diet is supplemented with vitamin B_{12}. How so? Contamination is regarded here as something to be avoided. The idea of a few mice-pellets in a vegetable soup is abhorrent, and grub-infested grain would be rejected with revulsion. Yet, it seems certain that this is how the Indian vegan gets his vitamin B_{12}.

Contamination may ruin or may improve the flavour of food. Flavouring substances are, of course, only present at levels of fractions of parts per million or even per 100 million, yet they may add greatly to our pleasure in eating. As a boy, I enjoyed home-churned butter sent to my parents by farmer friends. It

C

was delicious. Nowadays our butter is insipid stuff—adequate, nutritious and free from pathogenic bacteria. Yet it does not tempt me to eat bread and butter simply for its flavour as did the butter of my youth. This is not merely middle-aged deterioration of my taste-buds. It's much more likely that the milk in the churn was richly inoculated from the near-by farm midden. Contamination may be soundly conceived. Equally it may be a deadly danger.

Now I have pointed out the difficulties of defining the terms food, additive and contaminant to draw attention to the difficulties we encounter when we try to impose legal restrictions on their use. You cannot legislate until you define the terms with which you impose sanctions. It is an unfortunate but serious dilemma that words change their meaning with time and usage. Our system of law in the United Kingdom stretches back for century upon century. Legal terms have special and unique meanings set partly by precedent and partly by the Interpretation Act of 1889. This form of systematics has served the country well in the realms of criminal and civil law. Nowadays the lawyer has to deal with technical and scientific matters in addition to his accustomed territory. To depart from his semantic systematics, built up so laboriously over 1,000 years and with such loving care by Parliament, court of justice and legal library, would be unthinkable. Yet when the modern terminology of chemistry which also attributes unique meaning to its jargon meets the ancient terminology of law, trouble is to be expected. Science, the brash and confident newcomer, insists that its symbolism is unequivocal in interpretation and internationally understood. C_2H_5OH means the same to a Russian, a French, a British and an Eskimo scientist. Furthermore in six symbols it conveys a concept both of unique identity and quantitative composition. To the lawyer, there are 1,000 different drinks. In this simple formula the scientist gives you the glow of them all. Yet invite a lawyer to define what he means by alcohol and, in all likelihood, you will get 300 words of jargon comprehensible only to another lawyer. Even then, the precise meaning of the definition will only be settled after half a dozen test cases costing perhaps half a million pounds. Thus lawyers are rich and scientists are poor.

Yet behind this lies a dilemma which becomes increasingly

urgent as our society grows more complex. We cannot scrap the whole legal system to accommodate modern technology. Yet the pace of technical change forces us to deal with its hazards in ways which to laymen, scientists and lawyers alike seem increasingly incomprehensible, and unbelievably complex. In its present published form the law relating to manufacture and sale of food occupies two volumes[7] which together weigh about 9 lb.

I do not believe that any single person in the United Kingdom has all the ramifications of this system thoroughly at his finger-tips, yet the little Johnnie-a'-things shop at the corner is expected to obey it to the letter. Furthermore, it changes in detail on average about once a month. To be even moderately competent in this subject is a full-time job. The Ministry of Agriculture, Fisheries and Food has to maintain a whole staff of civil servants, lawyers and scientists to keep themselves up with it. They manage by parcelling it out in bits. The remainder of this chapter is largely concerned with how the system works at all, and with its enforcement which is officially done by the courts but which, in practice, is operated by what amounts to legalised blackmail. The fact that all this works, in the main, to the public good is a remarkable tribute to British law, to British adaptability and to British justice.

THE HISTORICAL SETTING

The use of chemical additives to food is an ancient practice, whose origins are lost in the dawn of recorded history. Wine, after all, is merely fruit juice preserved by alcohol, and the virtues of salt, saltpetre, sugar (in the form of honey) and the fumes of burning sulphur in extending the storage life of food were well-known to the Romans over 2,000 years ago. These simple methods of preservation were gradually refined through centuries of experience and the virtues of wood smoke as a preservative doubtless arose as a result of early attempts to dry meat over wood fires.

However, the chemical approach to food preservation was harmless enough until the rapid growth of the science of chemistry in the early nineteenth century made a more sophisticated approach possible. Unfortunately, if not un-naturally, new chemical knowledge fell into the hands of the unscrupulous, and was applied in the interests both of cheapness to the purchaser and of profit to the seller. But we must remember the social and economic background against which these developments were taking place. Members of my own generation recall the hard days of the slump of the early 1930's. We recall them as evil times which must not be allowed to occur again. But the worst days of the worst slump of this century are as nothing to the unbelievable conditions under which many of our peoples lived during the period 1800 to 1860. In England's green and pleasant land, children died of starvation, men and women lived in hovels under conditions of stinking squalor and sordidness, while the wealthy could command the autocratic power which stemmed from the common man's fear of want for himself, for his wife and for his family. If you think I paint too gloomy a picture, you can discover the facts of the situation in John Burnett's account of his recent researches into the ills of that black period of our social history.[2] To a starving man anything which cheapened the price of his meagre supply of food was to be welcomed.

The stage was set for the operations of the adulterers of food who called the growing knowledge of chemistry to their aid. At first, sophistication was a simple business. Bones were ground to a fine powder and mixed with flour, but other forms of adulteration of a more hazardous kind soon followed. Copper was added to beer, iron filings to tea, alum to bread. Dangerous substances such as formaldehyde were used as preservatives. Food was often coloured by the addition of toxic salts of heavy metals such as antimony, lead, copper and arsenic, and this was particularly dangerous when cheap confectionery, an occasional treat for the children of the poor, was made to look attractive by the addition of these chemicals.[3]

When several early scientists began to find adulterants of this sort in their studies of the composition of commercially available foodstuffs, there appears to have been a systematic conspiracy to suppress their evidence. There were violent outbreaks of criticism of their work as well as threats of violence which only the more courageous were able to sustain. Some published their data anonymously for fear of reprisal from the adulterers, while others, notably a Mr Accum[1] and a Dr Hassall[5] added their names to their published reports. At last even the *Lancet*, that most respectable of medical journals, came to their support. At this, Parliament was forced to act, and after a struggle lasting over 50 years in all, the first Food and Drugs Act was passed in 1860, to be followed 12 years later with a second Act, furnished with sharper teeth. The days of indiscriminate adulteration were over, and an effective system of inspection by public analysts and food inspectors properly qualified and equipped for the tasks they had to perform was established throughout the country. Despite certain shortcomings, this system persists to this day. It was a great achievement, yet it was only the first step in a process which has been developing ever since and which is yearly placed under greater stresses as the pace of scientific inventiveness increases.

THE PRESENT POSITION IN THE UNITED KINGDOM

A much travelled friend of mine once described Germany as a country in which everything which is not forbidden is permitted, Austria as a country in which everything is permitted which is not forbidden, and France as one in which everything is permitted which is forbidden. As already stated, in detail British food legislation is in a state of constant change but is steadily, and as an act of deliberate policy, moving to a position in which anything which is not permitted is forbidden. In other words, the Food and Drugs Acts of 1955 and 1956, together with the innumerable regulations made under powers granted the Ministries under the Acts, coupled with sundry other Acts are being systematically used to draw tighter and tighter bonds around what may be added to or abstracted from commercial foodstuffs. Curiously enough there are even important situations in which, by law, chemicals must be added to foods. To attempt to describe in any detail the operation of the law itself is far beyond the scope of this paper.

Chemicals added to food serve one or another of four main functions. They may be used:

(*a*) To improve the nutritional value of food. For example, bread flours must be fortified with calcium and iron and must conform to certain minimum requirements of B-group vitamin levels. Margarine must have minimum levels of vitamins A and D, which are similar to those in butter.

(*b*) To improve colour or flavour. This is often a target of attack by purists but food is nutritionally valueless if it is not attractive enough to be eaten.

(*c*) To improve texture or general appearance. This includes a large group of substances which are used to thicken sauces and gravy, to act as raising agents in baking, to act as agents retaining solids in suspension in, for example, soft drinks based on fruit juices, to prevent caking of hygroscopic powders, to glaze the tops of pies or buns, to emulsify fats and so on. There are traditional 'natural' substances suitable for all or most of these functions. There are also modern sophisticated versions of traditional materials. At first sight most people would react to the traditional cream of tartar and baking soda as a chemical raising agent for cakes as completely harmless, but would look with some suspicion on a more sophisticated modern equivalent. I suppose that this attitude is because their mothers used baking soda and cream of tartar in the kitchens of their youth. Yet we now know that toxicologically speaking tartaric acid is not above suspicion.[10]

(*d*) To improve the technological properties of food. This group includes substances which increase storage life such as preservatives and anti-oxidants, bleachers and improvers in bread and flour, acidifiers, bases or buffers used to adjust food pH values for technological reasons, solvents used as vehicles for other additives such as flavouring substances, surface-active and other agents used to improve the technological properties of fats, and so on. The use of such substances is often criticised on the grounds that their function is to help the manufacturer rather than the consumer. However, this kind of argument cuts two ways. Without this use, some basic foods would be much more expensive (bread is an example) while others would not be available at all. The end result would be higher food costs and a restriction of variety in diet.

Chemical contamination of food can arise in a range of ways. Agricultural chemicals used on the farm may be incorporated into food through the roots or leaves of plants and as a result every reader of this book has traces of D.D.T., B.H.C., aldrin and dieldrin in their body fat. During harvesting and storage on the farm there may be further contamination by rodents or insects; farm products such as milk may be contaminated by chemicals used for veterinary purposes on the cows. During factory processing there are further possibilities of contamination from lubricants used for food machinery, metals or the plastics with which the food inevitably comes into contact, and so on: finally chemicals may gain access to food from the packaging materials with which the food is wrapped.

The responsibility for advising the U.K. government of the day on these matters lies with the Food Additives and Contaminants Committee. This committee draws evidence on the numerous issues which fall within its terms of reference from a large number of sources, and in particular from the Laboratory of the Government Chemist on levels of contamination observed moving into food chains. I have mentioned agricultural residues, a topic on which there was public unrest three or four years ago. There are traces of these residues in our foods, the highest levels being found in mutton fat. It may be reassuring to mention that, supposing somebody wanted to use this fact to commit suicide, I have calculated on the known levels and known toxicity data that he would have to eat about five tons of mutton fat at a single sitting to do so. Modern methods of analysis are so incredibly sensitive that some of these substances can be detected and measured at levels down to about one part in 1,000 million parts of food. In round figures that represents 1 mg per ton.

The committee draws evidence on toxicity from a special panel of pharmacologists who collect and collate data from all over the world on possible hazards associated with chemicals which may appear in foods by accident or design. The total intellectual effort devoted to this topic is considerable and membership of the Food Additives and Contaminants Committee is a very demanding job in terms of the study required by each participant before a decision is reached on a given issue. Monthly meetings are held and it is not uncommon for members to be faced with reading and digesting anything from 20 to 100 pages of closely typed foolscap between meetings. At the same time the work is of tremendous scientific interest, and in this sense service on the committee is a very rewarding duty.

The committee has published guide-lines as to the general

standards of evidence it expects when chemical manufacturers and food processors submit an application for authority to use a new additive in food. Firstly, they must convince the committee that there is a need for the substance. Claims of need often break down on close inspection. Secondly, if need is established, the committee must be given evidence of safety-in-use of the substance concerned. Hard evidence of toxicological experiments is demanded. For example, to claim that a chemical additive is safe on the grounds that it is a naturally occurring substance, even one which is found in foodstuffs, is seldom acceptable. Oxalates (and many other toxic substances) occur naturally in foods. We do not wish to add to nature's bounty in this respect. Even when this second hurdle has been surmounted, the committee is mindful that the law must be administered. It therefore must be satisfied that analytical methods are available for the detection of the additive in food and that the substance proposed is of determinate chemical composition. Often, for example, emulsifiers of mixed chemical character are submitted, and these are looked on with disfavour because of the difficulty in ensuring that their use is not abused.

In all the argument which can be applied to these situations, (and on a decision of this committee thousands or even millions of pounds may hang in the balance) experience shows that criteria of absolute safety do not exist. Whatever is done, and whatever decision is made, an element of risk remains. If it is said that no chemical additives or contaminants will be permitted a far greater risk to the nation's well-being may result than if their use had been permitted. To forbid chemical additives and contaminants would be to forbid the use of wrapping materials to protect food from bacterial contamination, and to forbid the use of harmless preservatives to restrain otherwise unavoidable bacteriological deterioration.

Thus we conclude that while pure food is an unattainable ideal, clean, healthy and nutritious food depends on compromise, on balancing one set of risks against another, so that the practical level of risk is as small as human ingenuity can make it. Of course, scientific judgment is as subject to error as any other form of judgment, but error can be minimised in two ways—firstly by using every ascertainable fact at one's disposal and secondly by searching for generalised concepts as a guide to direction of judgment.

It is all very well to be philosophical about scientific judgments but to have to face the problems of an actual situation is salutary. Let us take the example of the widespread use of plastic films for wrapping foods. Many of their advantages are manifest. They protect the food but the customer can still inspect her purchase. Others are more subtle. These films are available in such a wide range of forms that their properties of vapour and gas permeability can be matched with accuracy to the technological function they are to perform. Yet in making them, the plastics industry uses hundreds of chemical substances for most of which no toxicological data exist. Now this would not matter if the plastics were chemically inert. This is far from being the case. Some are known to have constituents soluble in the food they protect and their solubility differs from one kind of food to another.

Now, suppose a tough line were to be taken on this problem. Suppose we said that no chemical was to be used in plastics for food use without adequate toxicological testing, we would have to test hundreds of chemicals, each test taking a minimum of two years to carry out and costing anything up to £50,000. Not only would this be absurdly expensive but there is not the skilled manpower in the United Kingdom to tackle a job of this magnitude. Furthermore, such a demand would divert existing skills away from more urgent work on, for example, drug metabolism and testing.

It is pertinent to remind the reader that while we certainly cannot say that there is no risk in the use of plastics, we can say that we do not know of any thoroughly authenticated evidence of poisoning having arisen from their use to date. At the same time our children will be exposed to their use from birth to death. Who can say that prolonged exposure to the extracted chemicals is without hazard? Clearly some control is necessary. How can it be applied in the public interest without hindering technological innovation? At the moment there are no legal controls in the United Kingdom although these do exist in some other countries. How can a problem of this level of complexity be dealt with through our archaic legal system? Clearly some simplifying concept is required.

It should now be clear that there are enough toxic substances of natural origin in the foods we consume to validate supposition that our bodies can dispose of small amounts of even quite highly toxic substances without harm of any sort of which we are aware. Had we some measure of the limits of this tolerance, we might arrive at a reasonable basis of decision. So far as I know the only attempt at such an estimate is that due to an American called John Frawley,[4] whose analysis has become dignified by the title 'The Frawley Concept'.

Frawley spent the early part of his career as a scientist in the service of the United States Food and Drug Administration. There he became sensitive to the absurdity of attempting to legislate comprehensively for all possible situations which might arise through the contamination of food with extraneous substances. For example, by 1966 the United States regulations governing chemicals used in food packaging (and which therefore might be transferred in traces to the food itself) contained 43,000 words listing (in one schedule alone of the 94 regulations) some 3,800 chemicals. Of these lists he was later to write 'Unless you work with these regulations on a daily basis and have sufficient technical training . . . it is almost impossible to determine the approved uses of a given chemical'.

He later left the United States Food and Drug Administration and joined the Hercules Company where he carried out one of the most thorough experimental investigations ever attempted of the migration of chemicals to foodstuffs from, not plastics or anything so sophisticated, but ordinary wrapping papers. As a result of these studies he concluded that anything which is present in a food container or coating at levels of less than 0·2% is safe beyond all reasonable doubt. Three-quarters of all the vast American legislation on packaging is superfluous if this statement is correct. The detail of his case is beyond the scope of this essay. I find it convincing. But convincing or not, there can be no doubt whatsoever that packaging is one of the most important single factors in protecting food from bacterial contamination. If packaging materials contribute to chemical contamination of food and if, at the same time, they contribute in a major way to the protection of food from bacterial contamination, a balance of risk must be struck. Where does the balance lie?

Up to the end of 1967, the U.K. Public Health Laboratory Service published an excellent little bulletin which, amongst other useful data, contained annual summaries of all recorded outbreaks of food poisoning in England and Wales. The figures for the last three years of publication are as follows:

1964	All cases	8,784
	Cases of chemical contamination	1
1965	All cases	11,317
	Cases of chemical contamination	84
1966	All cases	9,975
	Cases of chemical contamination	3

In the face of this kind of evidence it is clear that anyone faced with the responsibility of advising on food legislation must balance one kind of risk against another. All the data show that the risks of bacterial food poisoning are overwhelmingly important while those from chemicals are trivial. If an infinitely small risk from chemicals will reduce or avert a substantial hazard from food-borne diseases, let us by all means use chemicals.

In the affluent society our major hazards stem, not from chemicals in food, but from dirty food. If those who use media of mass communication to worry the public about chemicals in food, would devote equal energy and effort to clean up our systems of food handling and improve our standards of food hygiene they could change their role from scaremongers to that of public benefactors, for this is where the real hazards lie.

REFERENCES AND FURTHER READING

1. Accum, F., 1820. *A treatise on the adulterations of food and culinary poisons.* London.
2. Burnett, J., 1966. *Plenty and want.* Nelson, London.
3. Drummond, J. C. and Wilbraham, Anne, 1939. *The Englishman's food,* pp. 340-348. Jonathan Cape, London.
4. Frawley, J. P., 1967. *Scientific evidence and common sense as a basis for food packaging regulations.* Paper presented to the British Industrial Biological Research Association Annual Scientific Meeting. London.
5. Hassall, A. H., 1855. *Food and its adulteration.* London.

6. National Academy of Sciences, 1966. *Toxicants occurring naturally in foods*. Publication 1354, National Academy of Sciences, Washington, D.C.
7. O'Keefe, J. A., 1968. *Bell and O'Keefe's sale of food and drugs*, 14th ed. Butterworth, London.
8. Pyke, M., 1968. *Food and Society*. John Murray, London.
9. Winitz, M., Graff, J., Gallacher, N., Narkin, A. and Seedman, D. A., 1965. Evaluation of chemical diets as nutrition for man-in-space. *Nature*, **205**, 741.
10. WHO/FAO Expert Committee on Food Additives, 1966. *9th report*. WHO, Geneva.

H. J. EVANS

The genetic effects of contaminants

So far in these chapters we have considered the consequences of man's affluence on various aspects of human society, and the authors have, either directly or indirectly, frequently referred to the fact that the human species is contaminating its own environment and of course the environment of the plants and animals upon which man is so utterly dependent. In this chapter we shall briefly consider certain of the genetic effects of some of these contaminants, particularly on the human genetic system.

Alterations or mutations in the genetic materials occur spontaneously at a low rate and these mutations are of course a prime source of variation—the variation being fundamental to the process of evolution. In the case of a highly developed organism such as man, the vast majority of mutations will be harmful. This follows because mutations are continuously occurring, and have occurred throughout the history of man and his predecessors, so that all mutations which yield an advantage to an individual have been selected for and retained in the population, whereas deleterious mutations naturally die out with the individuals possessing them, the mutant individuals leave less offspring and so on. The real point here is that most of the so-called 'good' mutations that can occur have already occurred at one time or another so that the majority of newly induced ones must be bad.

The kinds of mutations that can occur can be grouped into two broad categories:

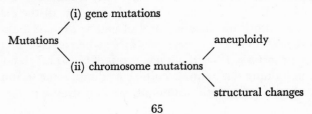

65

(i) GENE MUTATIONS

Gene mutations are changes within a single piece of information or gene and single gene mutations in man are responsible for a wide variety of clinical conditions. A good, but fortunately rare, example is Huntington's Chorea. These gene mutations occur spontaneously at a low rate—something around once in about 10^5 or 10^6 germ cells for a given gene—but here we must remember that in man each germ cell has some 40,000 or so genes. However, the frequency of such gene mutations is very much increased on exposure to physical mutagens such as ionising radiations, and chemical mutagens such as mercury or LSD—mutagens that are in fact contaminants of our environment and which are increasing in both variety and concentration.

(ii) CHROMOSOME MUTATIONS

Chromosome mutations can themselves be divided into two sorts: those resulting in a change in the number of chromosomes in all or some of the cells of an individual (aneuploidy) and those that result simply in a change in structure of one or more of the chromosomes. Both of these types of chromosome mutations occur in man and their frequency can be enormously increased on exposure to chemical mutagens or to radiations. Moreover, chromosome mutations in human somatic cells are amenable to study and for this reason I wish to devote most of my space to discussing this type of mutation. However, before discussing these chromosome mutations, let us first of all consider the normal human chromosome complement and the techniques that we use to look at man's chromosomes.

As a result of developments made over the last five or six years we can now make chromosome preparations from human peripheral blood leucocyte cells using only fractions of a millilitre of blood. In a normal individual virtually all the cells in blood are mitotically inactive and of course the chromosomes inside the cell nuclei only become visible when a cell undergoes division or mitosis. If we put a few drops of blood into a culture vessel containing some simple culture medium, some serum and a tiny amount of mitotic stimulant, we can stimulate the cells to undergo mitosis. This stimulation process takes a couple of days, so after two days in culture we have a population of dividing human cells in the culture vessel. We can subject these cultured cells to fairly standard cytological procedures and end up with microscope slides containing a few hundred dividing cells, each with their chromosomes beautifully spread out.

In normal man the number of chromosomes in the somatic cells is 46 so that 23 are present in the germ cells—the sperm and egg. The 46 chromosomes therefore are really 23 pairs, one of each pair being donated to the individual by his father and the other through his mother. These chromosomes contain all the information—all the genes—necessary to produce a normal

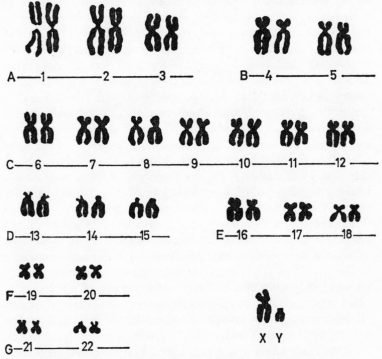

Figure 1. The chromosome complement of a normal male. The chromosomes in the peripheral blood white cell were photographed and then cut out from the photographic print with scissors and arranged in pairs. The chromosome pairs can be arranged into seven groups, A to G, on the basis of their morphology.

individual. One of these 23 pairs of chromosomes is concerned
with the inheritance of sex and in the male the two chromosomes
of this pair are dissimilar in size and in gene content and are
labelled X and Y, whereas the sex chromosomes in the normal
female are always homologous and are XX. For convenience
the chromosome complement of the normal male is referred to
as 46,XY and the normal female as 46,XX (Figure 1).

(a) Aneuploidy

The mutations that result in the condition of aneuploidy
imply a loss or gain of one or more chromosomes from the
normal diploid complement of 46. If this loss or gain occurs in
one or more somatic cells in an infant or an adult, it will be of
little consequence, but if it occurs in a germ cell or early on in
the development of an embryo then its consequences are usually
drastic. Unfortunately, aneuploidy is of relatively common
occurrence and it is responsible for a variety of congenital
anomalies. The commonest is known as Down's syndrome,
usually referred to as Mongolism, where the individual is
physically abnormal and is severely mentally handicapped.
Down's syndrome is the consequence of the presence of an
extra small chromosome (chromosome number 21, see Figure
2) so that the individual has 47 chromosomes in his/her body
cells (i.e. 47,XX or 47,XY). The incidence of Down's syndrome
in the general population is about 1 in 700 live births. Another
example of a rather less well-known anomaly is Klinefelter's
syndrome (47,XXY) where the individual has an extra sex
chromosome present and is an abnormal sterile male, sometimes
with some degree of mental impairment. Klinefelter's syndrome
is about half as frequent as Down's syndrome, but these are
unfortunately only two examples of a variety of viable aneuploid conditions. In very general terms we can say that the overall frequency of chromosomal anomalies of this kind in the
general population is such that about one in every 150 newborn
children is chromosomally abnormal. Moreover we know that
only a very small proportion of aneuploid embryos develop to
full term, since the mother's uterus acts as a fairly effective sieve
so that the majority of the chromosomally abnormal products
of conception are lost as early spontaneous abortions.

Our interest in these aneuploid conditions, from the point of

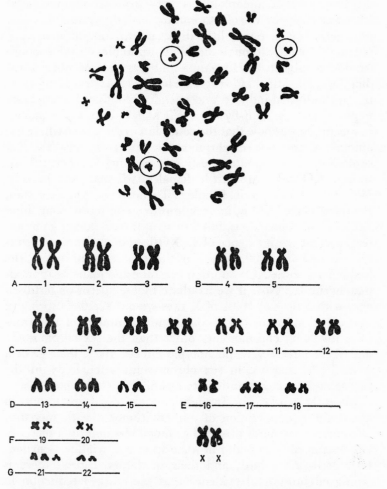

Down's syndrome. Trisomic for No 21.

Figure 2. Top: diagram of a metaphase cell from a female with Down's syndrome (47,XX). Bottom: the paired arrangements of chromosomes from the cell illustrated above. Note that there are five instead of the normal four G group chromosomes.

view of environmental contaminants, follows from the fact that
the frequency of aneuploidy is very dramatically increased
following exposure of cells to ionising radiations and chemical
mutagens. We have very little direct information on man himself on this point, although the follow-up studies on the A-bomb
irradiated subjects at Hiroshima and Nagasaki do not contra-
dict the expectation. However, we have a great deal of information on radiation-induced and chemically-induced aneuploidy
in plant cells, the fruit-fly *Drosophila* and, indeed, in the mouse.
For example we know that the condition in the mouse where the
animal has only one sex chromosome in its body cells (the XO
condition) occurs spontaneously in something like 7 in 10^3 offspring. XO mice are fertile females, whereas XO in man
(45,XO) gives the sterile female of Turner's syndrome. In man,
the incidence of XO is, in very approximate terms, something
like 8 in 10^3 conceptions, but 7 or so of these 8 do not go to full
term so that the incidence of 45,XO in the human newborn is
around one in 2,000. Thus, at the time of conception, the
frequencies of the XO condition in mouse and man are approximately similar. Now if we irradiate mouse sperm or fertilised
eggs with a dose of 100R of X-rays we get $32/10^3$ offspring of
the XO constitution and of course quite a number of abnormalities involving chromosomes other than the sex chromosome
and these have severe phenotypic effects. 100R then gives a
4 to 5-fold increase in sex chromosome aneuploidy in the
mouse and we might anticipate a similar effect in man.

Recently, workers in Sweden have expressed great concern
about the contamination of our environment with mercury.
Mercuric compounds are used as fungicides and high mercury
contents have been found in some species of wildlife—particularly seed-eating birds and their predators. Indeed there is
strong circumstantial evidence that the marked reduction in
population density of such birds as the yellow bunting, the
kestrel and the peregrine falcon in Sweden is a result of primary
or secondary poisoning from the extremely toxic organic alkyl-
mercurials. Similarly, high mercury contents (methyl mercury)
have been noted in fresh water fish such as the pike—and these
have been derived from industrial effluents discharged into
rivers.

Certain mercury compounds are extremely toxic to man and

have a very slow turn-over rate in the body. However, aside from its general toxic properties, what is not widely realised is that mercury is a mutagen and is a potential genetic hazard. For instance, in *Drosophila* in which, as in man, males are XY and females XX, exposure to methylmercury hydroxide at levels well below the standard toxicity levels (a few p.p.m.) results in increasing the frequency of XO and XXY individuals (analogous with Turner's and Klinefelter's syndromes in man) by up to a factor of five. Although we have not yet carried out direct tests on the effects of mercury on human cells in culture, past experience would suggest that similar results may be expected in man.

(b) Chromosome structural changes

In addition to inducing aneuploidy or a change in chromosome number, radiations and chemical mutagens also produce alterations in chromosome structure. Chromosome structural changes (or aberrations) occur spontaneously at low frequency and they are the most frequent alterations produced in chromosomes by mutagens. These changes arise as a consequence of breaks being produced in the chromosome threads of cells exposed to a mutagen (Fig. 3).

When a chromosome is broken the broken ends usually, but not invariably, rejoin so that the chromosome is repaired. In a proportion of cases the broken ends do not join back, so that a fragment of chromosome is produced that is not linked to a centromere (the locomotory organelle of the chromosome). Such an acentric fragment is not pulled to the poles of the cell when the cell divides so that it is excluded from the daughter nuclei produced as a result of mitosis. Cells with such breaks will therefore yield progeny cells that will be deficient for a certain amount of genetic material and will be mutant. If the deletion involves a loss of important genetic material, then the mutation may be lethal and kill the cell. If two or more breaks are present in a cell, then broken ends of one chromosome can join up with broken ends from another chromosome. Such an exchange could result either in an abnormal linking of chromosomes so that a structure with two centromeres (a dicentric) is formed, or to a transfer of genes from one chromosome to another (symmetrical translocation). If two breaks are produced

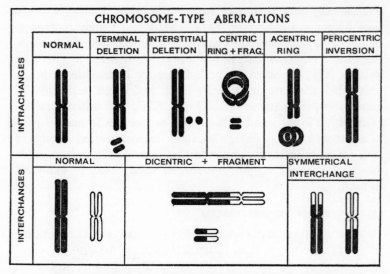

Figure 3. A diagrammatic representation of the chromosome-
type aberrations that may be induced in human blood cells
following a radiation exposure. The intrachange aberrations
are those that involve breaks and exchanges within a single
chromosome. Interchanges involve an exchange of parts
between chromosomes.

in the same chromosome—a not infrequent happening—then
abnormal rejoining will result in the formation of a ring
chromosome (see Fig. 3).

With the recent developments in techniques for examining
human chromosomes, we have over the last few years been able
to study chromosome aberrations in human cells in some detail.
We have been particularly interested in studying the effects of
irradiation on blood cells *in vitro* and have also studied cells in
blood taken from individuals exposed to radiation either as
part of their occupational hazard, or accidentally, or for therapeutic purposes. A typical picture of chromosome damage in an
irradiated human peripheral blood lymphocyte is shown in
Figure 4.

Many of the structural changes that I have referred to may
be quite viable in somatic cells, but are lethal if they are
present in the germ cells of the gonads. On the other hand if an
acentric fragment is not too large, then the genetic deficiency

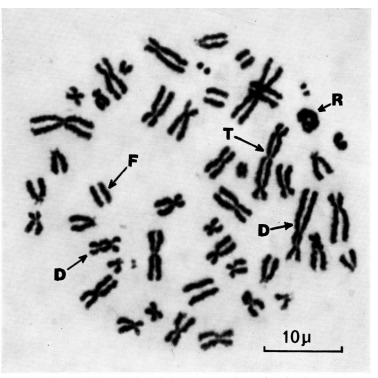

Figure 4. X-ray-induced chromosome aberrations in a human peripheral blood lymphocyte. The cell shows ten pairs of fragments (F), two dicentric (D), one tricentric (T) and one ring (R) chromosome.

that results from its loss may not influence the viability of a germ cell so this cell will carry a mutation. Similarly, symmetrical translocations may be viable and indeed spontaneously occurring translocations of this sort are responsible for a wide variety of congenital abnormalities. Evidence is accumulating that indicates that perhaps up to 1% of the population unknowingly carry a translocation and such translocations, which are usually physically quite harmless or of little direct consequence to the individual, are often a root cause of sterility.

In addition to the spontaneous occurrence of translocations, individuals possessing ring chromosomes and deficient chromosomes are well-known and can be exemplified by certain patients with Turner's syndrome who have one normal X chromosome and one ring X chromosome or a deficient chromosome.

There is one sort of chromosome deletion that I would like to refer to since it has implications with regard to radiation-induced leukaemia. To date something like 40 cases of chronic myeloid (granulocytic) leukaemia have been analysed chromosomally and these cases have been characterised by the presence of a deleted chromosome number 22. This deleted chromosome simply has a piece broken off its long arm and it is called the Philadelphia chromosome, since it was first reported to be associated with this type of leukaemia by a group working in Philadelphia. In typical cases a proportion of the blood cells and from 30 to 100% of the bone marrow cells contain this chromosome. When a patient is in remission, however, cells containing this chromosome are absent in peripheral blood but are still present—but to a lesser degree—in bone marrow. It is argued that this leukaemia is a direct consequence of this type of chromosomal change and it is worth noting that patients with Down's syndrome have an approximately 20-fold higher incidence of leukaemia than chromosomally normal individuals.

Now we know that radiation produces the sort of change that we see in the Philadelphia chromosome, and indeed six of the Japanese crew members of the *Lucky Dragon* fishing boat that were exposed to thermonuclear fall-out in the Pacific some years ago are now known to possess a Philadelphia-like chromosome in a small proportion of their cells; these individuals are being closely watched. Evidence from a variety of other sources has shown that radiation exposure can result in leukaemia. A survey involving a group of 'distinguished' (over 50 years of age) American radiologists showed that the leukaemia incidence in this group was 10 times higher than in other practitioners, and the survivors at Hiroshima and Nagasaki have also shown a 4 to 6-fold increase in leukaemia incidence over controls. Studies by Court Brown and Doll on leukaemia incidence in patients treated with X-ray therapy showed up to a 12-fold increase over controls. Moreover in this latter work it was shown that the incidence of leukaemia was strictly proportional to radiation dose, there being a linear relationship between the two parameters.

In addition to the leukaemogenic effect of mutagenic radiations, there are several chemical mutagens that have been implicated as causal agents in leukaemia and many chemical mutagens have been shown to be potent carcinogens in experimental animals. It seems not unlikely therefore that some human leukaemias may be a consequence of chromosome mutation, either arising spontaneously or as a consequence of exposure to mutagens.

So much for some of the obvious consequences of chromosome mutations: let us now turn to the question of how sensitive are man's chromosomes, or to put it the other way—how frequent are these events.

Using the peripheral blood culture technique we have over the past four or five years been studying the response of lymphocyte chromosomes to irradiation *in vitro*. The technique has simply involved either irradiating freshly drawn whole blood or irradiating blood in culture. The cells are cultured until they pass into division and cells in their post-irradiation mitosis are analysed for chromosome damage. The results of a typical experiment using 240 kV X-rays are shown in Figure 5. The data in this figure refer only to the clearly distinguished asymmetrical aberration types and these constitute one-half of the total aberrations induced. Our results show us that with an X-ray dose of 35 rads about 10% of the cells contain a structurally changed chromosome and at 200 rads there is a mean yield of one aberration per cell—and these of course are the asymmetrical aberrations. In fact in our experiments we can

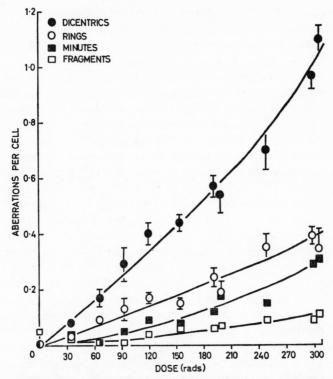

Figure 5. The relationship between X-ray dose and the yield of chromosome structural changes in human peripheral blood lymphocytes exposed *in vitro*.

easily detect the effect of a dose of as low as 10 rads. Man's chromosomes are therefore very sensitive to radiation.

The fact that we can easily detect a radiation effect with the very small dose of 10 rads suggests that we might be able to detect chromosomal damage in people exposed to very low doses of radiation as a consequence of their occupation—and indeed we can. Individuals receiving cumulative doses of more than 3 or 4 rads per year have a small but clearly increased frequency of chromosome aberrations in their peripheral blood cells as compared with controls. Moreover, because of the long life time of the small lymphocyte in the body we can detect these aberrations many years after the original exposure of the individual. I should hasten to add at this point that the presence of a low level of aberrations in an individual's blood cells does not appear to have any special clinical significance—we all have some aberrations in our blood cell chromosomes. Very high levels, however, may be a different matter.

Our chromosomes are probably also sensitive to the effects of chemical mutagens, although at the moment we are really only just beginning to study the action of chemical mutagens in human cells. Recently there was considerable newspaper publicity over the possibility that the hallucinatory drug LSD-25 (lysergic acid diethylamide) produced mutations in man. The first suggestive evidence of this was the finding of a low but significantly elevated frequency of chromosome aberrations in blood cells of LSD users. In addition, subjecting normal cells to low concentrations of this drug in test-tube experiments also resulted in the formation of aberrations. Although there have been several conflicting claims, to date the bulk of the evidence would appear to indicate that LSD, or a contaminating impurity, does produce genetic changes and that these changes can be easily detected in the blood cells of 'users'.

In all experiments on the action of mutagenic agents we find that the incidence of mutations is strictly proportional to the dose of mutagen received: different species, however, show different sensitivities. In the case of radiation exposure we know that the human chromosome complement is quite sensitive to aberration induction. Indeed in man we anticipate that a dose of around 30 rads will double the spontaneous mutation frequency. A dose of radiation or of a chemical mutagen that will double the spontaneous mutation frequency may be of little consequence to the physical well-being of the exposed individual, but mutations in the germ cells are passed on to the offspring and it is the future generations that suffer. This is therefore clearly a case of 'the sins of the fathers . . .'.

In conclusion I would like to re-emphasise the fact that in contaminating our environment with mutagens we must not forget that we are not merely hazarding our own good health and existence but we may, if we are not careful, place in jeopardy the future of our offspring and indeed the whole human race.

FURTHER READING

Evans, H. J., 1962. Aberrations of chromosome structure induced by ionizing radiations. *Int. Rev. Cytol.*, **13**.

Evans, H. J., Court Brown, W. M., and McLean, A. S. (eds.), 1967. *Human radiation cytogenics*. North-Holland Pub. Co., Amsterdam.

Jacobs, P. A., Price, W. H. and Law, P. (eds.), 1970. *Human population cytogenetics*. Pfizer Medical Monographs 5, Edinburgh University Press.

United Nations Scientific Committee, *Report on the effects of atomic radiation*. 24th session, supplement No. 13 (A/7613). H.M.S.O., London.

MAGNUS PYKE

Affluence and the natural history of a political animal

The phenomenon which we are discussing is the fact that largely because we have applied science and scientific thinking to the affairs of human existence we have succeeded in building up a number of communities which are rich to an unparalleled degree. Yet, just as in the fable of Midas, they are not happy. And no one has succeeded in governing and controlling these highly technological, sophisticated and affluent groups. The Americans, the French, the British, the Japanese, the Russians —all are unstable organisations. The thesis which I shall now examine is that this instability and its consequent unhappiness arise from a failure to understand the biological principles underlying the natural history of the multicellular organisations which human nations are. It is comparatively easy to study a giant panda at the molecular level but lacking a proper understanding of the natural history of the species, neither Russian nor British biologists know how to make two affluent giant pandas live together happily.

THE INDIVIDUAL IS A CELL OF A MULTICELLULAR COLONY OF POLITICAL ANIMALS

In the modern age there has grown up a new way of looking at the world and of describing reality. This is the official and scientific view (and language) in contrast with the colloquial and earthy. 'A molecular conglomerate of polymerised hexose units interlocked with the complex of linked cynnamyl alcohol units comprising the diverse lignin molecules' may be a true description of fact to a chemist; but an equally true description for a non-chemist is to call the same phenomenon a piece of wood. Similarly, it is equally true to describe conditions in countries scattered half round the world in terms of a list entitled: 'Estimated *per capita* daily calorie and protein contents of

78

net foodstuff supplies in some developing countries as compared with the U.S.A. 1960-62',[2] as it is to go to Peru and Ceylon, Pakistan and Israel, the U.A.R. and Uganda—all of which are included in the table—and talk to the people and try to see the conditions in which they live and the motives upon which their food habits are based.

The first language, the precise scientific talk of '*per capita* daily calorie and protein content' and the official jargon about 'developing' and 'developed' countries, although it serves its purpose in dealing at some degree of precision with a certain narrow area of meaning, may lead to error because of its very narrowness. Before this language was invented, before there were such things as 'developing nations', it was necessary to talk about Turkey and the Ottoman Empire, learn something about distant Peru, and the tribesmen of Khartoum. This approach, while less tidy and not so readily classifiable as the present United Nations language, comprised a wider area of meaning. The classification of Nigeria in the list of countries ranged in order of the calculated energy value of the 'protein content of net foodstuff supplies' gives a different kind of information about the place and its people than that obtained by a traveller who has some more direct and widely-based knowledge of the Ibo and the Yoruba who live there. And the list of vitamins and mineral values of the average diet of the pygmies in the rain forests of the Congo, although it can be compared with the best scientific assessment of the nutritional requirements of the people, only gives a limited picture of the actual situation unless it is reinforced by a proper understanding of the highly sophisticated customs by means of which the pygmies maintain themselves admirably in balance with the environment of the forest and the surrounding Negroes in the territory where they live.[18]

That branch of biology dubbed nutrition, as it is taught, and as it is very often practised, is not enough to deal with want. It is not enough to analyse a diet, to examine its content of calories and protein, the thiamine and riboflavine, niacin and biotin in it, to count the milligrams of calcium and iron, and the micrograms of copper and iodine. Nutritional surveys are two a penny. Devotedly, the nutritionists carry out clinical studies[13] to assess the incidence of protein-calorie deficiency disease among children in Haiti and Brazil, Sicily and Andhara Pradesh. But even this does not fully describe the truth.

The dietary surveys show that the affluent United States is the best-fed country on earth.[2] The estimated *per capita* daily calories are 3,100, whereas the same survey shows that in Peru they eat only 2,230 calories. (By a statistical peculiarity, the survey shows the Japanese, too, as getting only 2,230 calories.) But how clear and vivid a picture do these seemingly precise quantitative and scientific figures give of the American situation?

'Nutritional deficiency diseases due solely to an inadequate diet have almost disappeared,' writes Dr G. A. Goldsmith of the School of Medicine, Tulane University.[4] 'The nutritional state of persons living in the United States is in general very good. We are fortunate in having an abundant and varied food supply. . . . Although primary nutritional deficiency diseases are now a rarity . . . we cannot afford to be complacent. The prevalence of obesity with its many hazards to health should concern all of us.'

These statements are true, the scientific evidence supports them. But just as a higher animal is made up of many types of living cells, the function and structure of some of which are different from those of others, yet each must be well if the being of which they are all part is to be healthy, so is a community made up of its constituent men and women who also may be of diverse types. If we turn, therefore, to a second American scientific observer, Dr Jean Mayer of the Department of Nutrition of Harvard University,[11] we find an account of evidence showing that among other United States citizens—Negro families in the Southern states—60% eat diets which are 'obviously inadequate'. 'While the calorie requirements are generally covered for all members of the family, the protein intake of the children tends to be only border-line. Calcium intakes are low in at least 25% of the population, perhaps as much as 35%, and iron intake is low in 12 to 15% of the population; vitamin A requirements are not adequately covered in as much as 80%; vitamin C intake is inadequate for much of the population, particularly the urban group, for several months of each year.'

This is one example of a group living within the main society

of the nation, yet separate from it; living in a richly endowed
land, yet cut off from its material wealth, and—more important
than this—isolated from its social endowment as well. And in-
comparably more deprived even than these wretched inhabitants of the Negro colonies, are the 'migrant streams' who, year
after year, like lost tribes for ever on the move, and numbering
tens of thousands of Puerto Rican and other 'Whites' as well as
Negro labourers and their families, follow the harvests from
Florida to upstate New York. Poor, barely educated, pursuing a
broken social existence, those people are of all others the most
unfortunate. Their food was found[1] to consist of flour and maize
grits supplemented by beans; the tails, feet, ears and neck-
bones of pigs; some chicken, fish and cheese; but practically no
milk. Their way of existence precluded almost any cooking.
Among them were found cases of scurvy, rickets, hunger oedema,
marasmus and kwashiorkor. And this in the wealthy United
States.

The nutritional statistics of America give no inkling of the
existence of these wretched people of the 'migrant stream'. 'It
is not unusual', writes Dr Mayer, 'for migrants to follow the
stream for ten or even twenty years.' Living in the wealthiest,
most lavishly provisioned land on earth, in which there are
proportionally more doctors and nutritional experts and
scientists than in any other country, their nutritional status is
worse by far than that of the Congo pygmies among whom
Turnbull[18] lived for more than a year. Yet the pygmies,
lacking supplies of vitamin-enriched breakfast food, and the
advice of the Food and Nutritional Board of the U.S. National
Research Council, enjoyed a complex and stable social system.
Their co-operative methods of hunting, of building houses of
branches and leaves, and, above all, their highly organised
marriage rituals and educational and legal arrangements—all
these contributed to the attainment of something nearly
approximating to the WHO goal of 'a state of complete physical,
mental and social well-being'. Compared with the Congo
pygmies, the health of the American citizens of the 'migrant
stream' was deficient indeed. But not so much deficient in
vitamin D and vitamin C, iron, protein and calories to which
their rickets and scurvy, anaemia, kwashiorkor and marasmus
can be attributed, as in the entire fabric of a tolerable social

system. 'Serial monogamy', the coupling of men and women from one to another as the tattered migrants shift from one set of plantation hutments to the next, denies the possibility of proper human existence. The cause of death of a man killed in a traffic accident can be attributed to his skull being fractured. Alternatively, the cause of death is equally due to the restless malaise that impels him to leave the noisy vacuity of his crowded home to drive to a boxing match in the next town. Welfare workers issuing vitamin tablets to the colonies of migrating labourers will not bring them to health.

THE NERVOUS SYSTEM OF A SOCIAL COMMUNITY

A multicellular organism possesses a communications system. Within this system information and knowledge are stored, learning takes place and wisdom accrues. Within the corporate body of a community similar systems of communication and learning—whether they are university courses or TV broadcasts—exist.

One of the most dramatic attributes of the current advance in scientific technology has been the development of means of communication. There are no parts of the world so remote that information cannot instantly be transmitted from them. There are no distances on earth so great that a representative from the United Nations cannot travel from New York, Rome, Geneva or Paris to be there the following day. And representatives from the United Nations technical agencies do in fact go. It is from their work and the statistics they collect from the governments of the territories they visit that the alarming statements about the number of people suffering from 'hunger'[16] are derived. But among the 50 or more countries who raise many millions of pounds to support a campaign for a 'final solution' of the food problems which beset the world, and among the welfare organisations in many lands, are those who have come to understand that problems of malnutrition cannot be solved either in 'developing' or 'developed' countries simply by supplying enough food.

Professor D. S. McLaren,[10] writing from the American University of Beirut, Lebanon, has pointed out that to say a population is suffering from 'hunger' may nowadays mean one of two different things. It may be a medical statement that people show signs of deficiency diseases, the diagnosis of which is confirmed when the diseases respond to dietary measures. Or it may be surveys of food consumption, a non-medical diagnosis based on showing that their food statistics do not come up to the official standards; this has somewhat fancifully been called 'hidden hunger'. When FAO put out their estimates that of the entire world population half to two-thirds are ill-fed, it is to 'hidden hunger' they refer.

It must be accepted that kwashiorkor and nutritional maras-mus, which form the subject of the harrowing illustrations with which Oxfam prods the consciences of charitable people, are responsible for the death of scores of thousands of children each year, and in their less severe manifestations contribute to the death of hundreds of thousands more, and blight the lives possibly of millions of others who survive. Again, it has been computed that somewhere about 20,000 children go blind every year from xerophthalmia, for lack of vitamin A in their diets; and this computation excludes China, from which no reliable information is available. In most developing countries nutritional anaemias cause much illness, and are a contributory cause of death particularly in infants and women during the child-bearing period. For the world as a whole, rickets, scurvy, beri-beri and pellagra—all diseases directly due to nutritional deficiency—are less important than they once were, but still take a significant toll of victims.

But will all these nutritional diseases, manifestations of what the official organisations call 'hunger', be done away with by supplies of food purchased with all these millions of pounds of money? For the most part they are diseases of infancy and childhood, and their cause is not lack of food, but lack of know-ledge or fixed behaviour based on one of the diverse human motives other than knowledge. 'At any moment, from Manila to Guatemala City and from Cape Town to Cairo,' wrote Professor McLaren, 'infants in their thousands are becoming sick and dying from kwashiorkor and its related syndromes—essentially due to lack of protein. The reason for their illness and death is nearly always maldistribution of protein within the family. The helpless toddler, often suddenly weaned when a new pregnancy is on the way, does not get his share. Fish, a major source of protein in Malaya, is prohibited to young children because it is believed to produce worms. Infections and infestations, often mistreated with semi-starvation diets of rice-water, barley-water, or weak tea, make his chances even poorer.'

On the green tropical island of Java, many hundreds of infants go blind and die for lack of a few milligrams of pro-vitamin A. Yet around them is all the carotene in creation—this same pro-vitamin A. Many green leaves are used for animal fodder, but are regarded as unfit for human consumption. Most south-east Asians consider rice—a commodity entirely devoid of carotene, and deficient as well in some of the essential amino acids without which kwashiorkor or some other calorie-protein deficiency disease may arise—the perfect supplementary food for infants. The structure of a human community is complex, and the inter-relationships by which its component parts are bound may be powerful and tense. An American ship-load of dried egg or a team of Dutch administrators would, considered on a strictly technical—some might say 'scientific'—basis, solve the problem of xerophthalmia in Java. In fact—and science is a pragmatic system that deals with facts—neither would of itself benefit the situation in an aggressively 'free' Indonesia.

Similar instances could be multiplied of communities in which people suffer, and health is damaged, not because the means are inadequate, but rather because the knowledge or the will is lacking. Education and thought can do much, but education for whom? Every Great Power, every 'developed' nation, every liberal journalist, and half the pulpits in Christendom shout their horror of 'hidden hunger' and hope for the time of a final solution when no one on earth will be hungry. Yet what does 'hidden hunger', which so blankets the statistical assessment of want, and confuses the issue of deficiency diseases, do to man? Does it kill, blind, or shorten life? Obesity certainly shortens life. Dr Sen, Director-General of FAO, says[16] that 'hidden hunger' leads to 'impaired vigour and lowered vitality and thus to idle hands', to 'prematurely ageing mothers and idle youth'. But we are not told how nutrient lack was proved to be the cause of 'impaired vigour', 'premature ageing', and 'idleness of youth'. What we do know is that millions of overfed people living in the developing countries of the world suffer the same ill-effects as ourselves, whilst their 'hidden hungry' brethren do not. Learning leads to knowledge, and thence, we must hope, to wisdom—alike for the demonstrably malnourished Javanese, to the Dutch administrators who know well that vitamins must take their place in the balance with political autonomy for Indonesia, both being components of the human situation, and for Dr Sen as well.

In Java the children suffer from malnutrition because the society of which they are a part lacks the knowledge of the vitamin A activity in the herbage around them. In the United States, pockets of the population are poor and hungry because the rich society of which they form a part does not know that they exist. Louis Heron[6] quotes a senior medical officer of one of the Great Society programmes as saying 'We know more about nutrition in Pakistan than we do in the United States'. Using the official government statistics and the official government definition of 'poverty', which carries within it the inherent implication (as did Rowntree's 'poverty line' in York in 1899) of inevitable hunger, the investigators of the Citizens Crusade[14] related the number of 'poor' people to the number receiving any relief from official programmes to supply the needy with food. In Connecticut, the second richest state in the Union, 236,220 people were found officially classified as 'poor'; only 4,945 were on the lists of those receiving free or cheap food. In South Carolina, 715,778 were 'poor', 10,878 were given help, and 17 out of 20 counties investigated had no programme of help at all. In the 15 Southern and border states, more than three million 'poor' people were found to whom no state welfare programme was available; of seven million others officially categorised as 'poor' and by definition in need of aid, aid was provided for one million.

Nutritional knowledge, for lack of which children may go blind and die, concerns the role of vitamin A and xerophthalmia. But no community wants children to suffer from malnutrition. When they do, the knowledge lacking may be partly that of the biochemical mechanism of vitamin A, and partly of the social mechanism which moves, for instance, the Javanese community to live as it does. Or, where eight or nine million Americans are poor and underfed, the knowledge lacking—certainly not that of nutritional science as taught at Harvard—

D

may be of the principles by which the behaviour of a community of men, some white, some black, some Puerto Rican, is
determined; and of how to learn to see the condition of one's
own body-politic, even though not all of it is healthy.

CONTROLLING THE SOCIAL ORGANISM

It is a salutary exercise for a biologist to stand back occasionally
and look with a clear eye at what his scientific knowledge can
do to insure the well being of the complex organisms of a human
community. Let us for a start consider just nutritional health.
The 'scientific' attack on world malnutrition is lacking in three
respects. First of all, knowledge of the biochemistry of nutrition,
detailed and effective though it has become in the last two
decades, is ineffective without equally complete scientific knowledge of human ecology—that is, how men behave in harmony
or in competition with other members of their colony, in relation
to the climate, the land, the cities they live in, and all the
environmental paraphernalia of twentieth-century life. The
second area of ignorance, which those who plan to apply
nutritional knowledge to practical affairs must at least recognise, is economics. The Affluent Society is not fully under the
intellectual control of those who run it, nor are all its citizens
affluent. Communities will continue to suffer from kwashiorkor,
due to inadequate supplies of protein for young children, even
if welfare organisations set up a factory to make fish flour, or
lay out plantations of groundnuts, should the indigenous population find it more profitable to sell the fish flour and the
groundnuts than to eat them. And the third reason why science
of itself is not enough is that international aid may be twisted by
the unclear motives of the donors.

When in the middle of the nineteenth century 'advanced'
countries began to adopt science as one of the basic philosophical principles upon which society should be run, Darwin's ideas
were seriously taken to apply to social conduct. The principles
of evolution were often expressed as the 'survival of the fittest'.
Man had only achieved his predominant position as head of
creation because he was fit to dominate and if he wished,
exterminate any other species. Within the community of mankind, therefore, it could equally aptly be argued that rich

successful men, and powerful and dominant trading nations, were successful, powerful and dominant because they were fitter than the others. A corollary of this argument was that to help poor, weak and unsuccessful people was foolish, unscientific and likely to hold back the progress of human evolution. As the nineteenth century gave way to the twentieth, this fundamental doctrine was gradually modified until in almost all educated communities—even the United States, where pure scientific thinking had been deeply entrenched—the idea of a welfare state emerged, and from this grew the present notion of the welfare world supported by the global association of the United Nations.

But parallel with the accepted principle that it was the duty of rich nations to give aid to poor ones, there grew up an equally loudly asserted doctrine that every nation, no matter how small, poor, ignorant and incompetent, had a right to its own absolute freedom to run its own affairs. These two tenets were given practical support by very large subventions of aid by the donor nations. For example, in 1944 the official aid expenditure of the United States was 3,534 million dollars, that of France 841 million dollars, and those of Great Britain and Germany 490 and 460 million dollars respectively.[12]

International aid comprises money, goods, food and technical advice. The Food and Agriculture Organisation and the World Health Organisation of the United Nations, as I have already mentioned, carry out nutritional and medical surveys in developing nations all over the world. The principal nations contributing aid, notably the United States, France, Great Britain and Germany, also provide technical and administrative advisers and, in addition, there are numerous foundations and charitable and religious organisations which go out from Western technological nations to advise and help those whom they consider to be less fortunate than themselves. Yet the philosophical observer of this massive deployment of dynamic benevolence may well ask whether it achieves the ends for which it is devised. The detribalising influence of the mercenary Western ethic may, by breaking up an existing closely knit social system, do more harm than good; and, by accustoming a community to the sophisticated products of Western technology, pauperise the people whom it was intended to help.

Considerable thought has been given to the effectiveness of aid as a means of achieving the economic development and hence, presumably, the improved nutritional status, of poor countries.[15] The results of such reflections show that effectiveness is uneven and the purposes for which the aid is given diverse. The French and the Americans are clear on two matters. The first is that they know better than the recipients what is good for them. Secondly, these two nations are candidly aware that, no matter how kindly their feelings are towards the 'have-not' nations, the reason for disbursing men and treasure in the form of aid is basically to benefit France and America. To a French official it is 'obvious' that by giving aid to a developing nation France is exerting influence. The American nutritionist, R. R. Williams, chairman of the Williams-Waterman Fund for the Combat of Dietary Diseases, found nothing incongruous in concluding an article on 'Chemistry as a supplement to agriculture in meeting the world's food needs'[19] with the words: 'Manufacturing chemistry can ultimately aid agriculture greatly by producing synthetically and selectively those essential components of food which are required in minor amounts. . . . The dominant peoples in whose hands now reside the scientific knowledge and technology of present-day earth are already outnumbered manyfold by the dark-skinned races in need of our help. If we do not aid them, Communism will surely attempt to do so and will use these people as cannon fodder to destroy us.'

Equally well-meaning, with equal knowledge of science, and fully as single minded, the Soviet Union also has launched out into a massive programme of loans and foreign aid. It has been estimated[17] that between 1954 and 1965 Soviet credits and grants extended to developing countries amounted to some $5,000 million. About 41% of this was spent in the Middle East, partly, no doubt, to improve the nutritional status of the Arab nations, but partly for reasons similar to those expressed by the chairman of the Williams-Waterman Fund for the Combat of Dietary Diseases.

'Reflecting on his voyages to Polynesia in the late eighteenth century, Captain Cook later wrote that "It would have been better for these people never to have known us. . . ." Even when acting with the best of intentions, Americans, like other Western peoples who have carried their civilisations abroad, have had something of the same fatal impact on smaller nations that European explorers had on the Tahitians and the native Australians.'[3] Scientists going into the 'hungry' countries to bring the benefits of nutritional science can deploy valuable knowledge provided they appreciate that they do not possess the whole of wisdom. In August 1967, the Fourth Rehovoth Conference held in Israel was devoted to health problems in developing States. The main theme running through the conference was that in planning health services and medical education, the new countries must not copy the patterns of the old—patterns which many of the old 'developed' nations themselves now realise to be far from ideal in the modern world. In an address which to a large degree summarises the intent of this paper, Dr M. G. Candau, Director-General of the World Health Organisation,[7] made a plea for an ecological approach in which man would be viewed as inseparable from his environment, his ancestry and his culture; and he called on countries that had emerged from colonialism to free themselves also from 'technological colonialism'. For one thing, the nutritional scientists, trained in biochemistry, physiology, food chemistry and clinical medicine, who come to colonise them, do not always know enough to achieve what they set out to do. McGonigle[9] years ago set out to help the poor, undernourished slum-dwellers of Stockton-on-Tees. His nutritional knowledge was in advance of his generation, his clinical acumen was outstanding, his science impeccable and his drive and force of character untiring. Yet when his work was done, and the unfortunate people of the town were rehoused in fine, new, sanitary dwellings, their health deteriorated and the death rate rose. The rents of their new houses were higher than those of the squalid tenements they had lived in before.

Molecular biology has been a potent intellectual force. Beri-beri was once a disease which scourged the East. It decimated the Japanese Navy; its victims in the Philippines, in Indonesia, Malaya, and Central America were numbered in tens of thousands; for want of a few grams of thiamine—obtainable today by the ton—a British army was compelled to surrender to the Turks at Kut-el-Amara.[5] The highly technical discovery of Lohmann and Schuster in 1937[8] that a diphosphate ester of vitamin B_1 functions as the co-enzyme, cocarboxylase—

lacking which pyruvic acid accumulates in the tissues and by its toxic effect causes the symptoms of beri-beri leading swiftly, if not relieved, to death—was the key to the relief of mankind from beri-beri. Without this scientific knowledge, British generals, Japanese admirals and the Dutch administrators of the Orient were helpless. But because he possesses it, the nutritional scientist is not equipped to solve the problems of developing nations abroad, nor even those of Stockton-on-Tees at home. It can now quite clearly be seen that the scientists guiding governments and their administrators, charitable organisations and missionaries, and the special agencies of the great United Nations alike, need a new kind of approach to the situations with which they set out to deal. These situations are part of the natural history of man.

A man equipped to deal with human natural history must have at his command a proper knowledge of nutrition and of economics, agriculture and the dozen or more of scientific disciplines which apply to the complexity of the scientific age in the twentieth century. But even to appreciate the usefulness of these sciences, and the depth of scholarship which they now provide, is not enough. The Admirable Crichton whom we now need to cope with the poor and starving people of the modern world must also appreciate the limitation of science. The molecular biologist may rightly understand the nature of DNA, the molecule controlling genetical inheritance, without being in the least able to arrange to manufacture a Michelangelo, or, indeed, without possessing any very clear idea about what sort of person he would choose were he able to produce such a person at will. The natural historian may understand the factors causing malnutrition in Egypt—lack of B-vitamins, lack of calories, intestinal worms, lack of industrial development, and hatred of Israel—without fully knowing how to remedy the situation.

The flowering of scientific discovery and its application to practical affairs have constituted one of the major revolutions in the narrative of man. But the revolution has happened and is beginning to dwindle into the perspective of history. The biologist, when he leaves behind his frogs pickled in formalin, his cages of fruit flies, his electron microscope and his messenger RNA and takes it upon himself to study affluence must learn to be more than a scientist. He must strive to understand the natural history of man—the political animal.

REFERENCES

1. Browning, R. H. and Northcutt, T. J., 1961. On the season: a report of a public health project conducted among negro migrant agricultural workers in Palm Beach, Florida. *Florida Bd. of Health Monograph*, N. 2.
2. FAO, 1965. *Production year book*. FAO, Rome.
3. Fulbright, J. W., 1967. *The arrogance of power*. Jonathan Cape, London.
4. Goldsmith, Grace A., 1965. Clinical nutrition problems in the United States today. *Nutrition Rev.*, 23, 1.
5. Heher, C., 1917. *Mesopotamia Commission Rept.*, appendix III.
6. Heron, L., 1967. *The Observer*, London, June 20th.
7. *Lancet*, 1967. (Annotation) Health in developing countries, 2, 551.
8. Lohmann, K. and Schuster, P., 1937. Cocarboxylase.*Naturwissenschaften*, 25, 26.
9. McGonigle, G. C. A. and Kirby, L., 1936. *Poverty and public health*. Gollancz, London.
10. McLaren, D. S., 1963. World hunger: some misconceptions. *Lancet*, 2, 86.
11. Mayer, Jean, 1965 .The nutritional status of American Negroes. *Nutrition Rev.*, 23, 161.
12. Organisation of Economic Co-operation and Development, 1965. *Development assembly efforts and policies*. Rev. Paris.
13. Patwardhan, W. N., 1964. Protein-calorie deficiency disease: public health aspects. In: Mills, E. F. and Passmore, R. (eds.). *Proc. VI. Int. Congress Nut.*, *p*. 310. Livingstone, Edinburgh.
14. Report of the Citizens Crusade against Poverty; Ford Foundation and CIO, New York 1967.
15. Report of int. conf. of Ditchley Foundation and Overseas Development Inst. *Effective aid*. ODI, London, 1966.
16. Sen, B. R., 1966. *State of food and agriculture 1966*. FAO, Rome.
17. *The Times*, 1967. (Report) p. 8, London, Sept. 26th.
18. Turnbull, C. M., 1961. *The forest people*. Simon and Schuster, New York.
19. Williams, R. R., 1956. Chemistry as a supplement to agriculture in meeting world food needs. *Amer. Sci.*, 44, 317.

FURTHER READING

Bridger, G. and de Soissons, M., 1970. *Famine in retreat*. Dent, London.
Pyke, M., 1968. *Food and society*. John Murray, London.
Pyke, M., 1970. *Man and Food*. Weidenfeld & Nicholson, London.

The editors acknowledge their gratitude to Messrs John Murray (Publishers) Ltd. for permission to use material in the above chapter which has appeared in Dr. Pyke's book *Food and society* published by them and referred to above.

SIR DUGALD BAIRD

Affluence and the birth rate

There is a strong element of stability in Nature. Most animals maintain a population on a fairly constant level; there are fluctuations of numbers, but they are fluctuations round a mean. How is the population fixed at this relatively stable level? Some say that the rules of Malthus apply strictly to the animal world—starvation, disease and predators are the stabilisers. Others, for example Professor Wynne Edwards, say that animals limit their numbers before starvation does it for them. It is part of the animal's social organisation.

In Man high fertility was necessary to safeguard his survival in primitive societies where death rates were high and the expectation of life short, but if numbers and food supply got out of balance, systems of control, similar to those in animals, probably operated. The process of civilisation, however, has raised so many barriers between modern man and his environment (such as the sudden conquest of many diseases by modern antibiotics), that population control for him can only be based on his own conscious efforts. In underdeveloped countries the *sudden* great reduction in deaths from infections in the last 20 years, especially in children, has increased enormously the numbers reaching maturity and this in turn is resulting in a great increase in the number of babies born. It has given rise to what is well known today as the 'population explosion'. This should be checked by an immediate decrease in the number of births and in the average family size. We have the technical means to do it, but what we cannot do is to bring about a rapid change in the reproductive habits of men and women especially in underdeveloped countries where there are long-standing traditions acting in the other direction. A reduction in family size has occurred gradually with increasing industrialisation and improvement in living standards and education. The world problem is now generally realised to be urgent and so important that what amounts to emergency methods must be adopted. One of the difficulties is that any lowering of the birth rate may be nullified by a lower child death rate brought about by health education which accompanies family planning programmes.

Over the last 200 years in Europe the population has increased steadily as a result of falling death rates due to increasing affluence and consequently higher standards of living and of medical care. In Britain the birth rate remained high till 1870 when the passing of the Education Act made child education compulsory. Children were no longer an economic asset and in fact became the most common cause of poverty. The effect of the high death rate amongst young men in the First World War and the economic depression which followed it led to a sharp decline in the birth rate and the marriage rate and for the first time the net reproduction rate was less than 1, that is to say the birth rate was not high enough for replacement of the population. This led the Government to appoint a Royal Commission on Population to advise on the measures most likely to increase the birth rate. By the time it reported its findings the birth rate had already risen and has been maintained at a level well above replacement ever since.

The effect of the economic depression on the birth rate was greater in the upper than in the lower socio-economic groups of the population. Thus the net reproduction rate was 0·7 in the prosperous South-East of England and 1·4 in the depressed North. As a consequence a majority of children in those years were reared in a poor environment and were poorly grown and under-nourished. In these areas mortality rates from conditions associated with poverty, notably infant mortality, were excessive. The perinatal mortality rate (stillbirth + first week death rates) was high in the North and low in the South-East of England. In Scotland rates were highest in Glasgow and the other industrial towns in the Clyde valley. The National Birthday Trust Perinatal Mortality Survey in 1958 confirmed these geographical differences and showed that the high rates in the North were associated particularly with prematurity and malformations of the central nervous system of the foetus, conditions known to be predisposed to by poor social circumstances.

The Survey also confirmed the close association between

perinatal mortality and the health and physique of the mother. For example the perinatal mortality rate in tall primigravidae in the professional classes was 19 per 1,000 while in short women in the semi- and unskilled classes the rate was 49. In each social class the perinatal mortality rate rose as stature decreased. The most likely explanation of this is that in Britain today many women are short because they have not grown to their potential height. If the skeleton is not fully developed other organs of the body may also not have developed fully and thus will function less effectively than they should during pregnancy. Children are most likely to grow to their maximum height in the conditions which prevail in professional homes.

The percentage of women who are tall decreases from South to North in the U.K. In Aberdeen, and probably in Scotland as a whole, women are even shorter than in the North of England. It is well known that wage rates and standards of living generally are lower in Scotland than in England. Migration also has an effect on the average stature. Migration from Scotland has always been high. Our researches in Aberdeen have shown that those young mothers who leave Aberdeen within five years of the first birth (about 20% of the total) are taller, have lower perinatal mortality rates and are more intelligent than those who remain in the city.

Nevertheless the perinatal mortality rate in Aberdeen is as low as in the South of England. The most likely explanation is that the standard of obstetrics is much higher than average in Aberdeen. The perinatal mortality rate has fallen faster in Dundee and Aberdeen than in the larger Scottish cities, suggesting that the organisation of an efficient area service is easier in the smaller regions. However, we should never neglect the fundamental fact that the mother's reproductive efficiency is the most important factor affecting the outcome of pregnancy. For example, very good results have been achieved in Holland with a relatively simple service because of the very high level of health and physique of the population.

Britain today is affluent but stillbirth rates are still relatively high because of the damage done to the health of mothers by the living conditions brought about by the industrial revolution. Glasgow is possibly the clearest example, in Scotland at least, of how the benefits of affluence may have been restricted to the upper social classes and in fact may have caused deterioration in health and living conditions of the lower social classes. Glasgow has been notorious for chronic bronchitis, pulmonary tuberculosis and rickets. The smoke from coal fires, domestic as well as industrial, blotted out the sun and diets were grossly deficient in protein and vitamins. Other factors were over-crowding and substandard housing. Statutory overcrowding was four times greater than in any city in England. The birth rate was and still is characteristically high in such adverse conditions and Glasgow is no exception.

Legislation to deal radically with situations of this kind is usually enacted slowly in peace-time, but sometimes during the urgency of war more rapid progress can be made. For example at the beginning of the Second World War, and in large measure as a result of the work of Lord Boyd Orr and his associates at the Rowett Institute, the Government introduced an enlightened food policy which put mothers and young children in a high priority class for essential foods and this was accompanied by an intensive campaign about the importance of taking the rations allocated. The quality of the diets of the underprivileged sections of the population improved and this is thought to be largely responsible for the remarkable fall of 40% in the perinatal mortality rate between 1940 and 1948. In England and Wales the mortality rate fell most in South Wales where unemployment had been greatest and fell least in the South-East of England where the unemployment rate was comparatively low.

Another effect of the food policy and the concentration on health education was that children grew taller and on average became considerably taller than their parents. The consequent improvement in the reproductive efficiency of young mothers today is one of the factors responsible for the decline of 30% in the perinatal mortality rate which occurred between 1958 and 1967. Another factor is that now most women are younger at the time of the birth of their first baby. They thus have the two essentials for easy and efficient childbearing—youth and health. In regard to perinatal mortality rates we are catching up with Holland, Norway, Denmark and Sweden where these require-ments have been met by the childbearing population for many years. The fact that a low perinatal mortality rate is not merely a matter of the Gross National Product is demonstrated by Norway where the G.N.P. is not high and wages and salaries are comparatively low, but by enlightened social policies, the basic needs for health seem to be within the reach of almost everyone.

Not surprisingly the improved education of the young today has caused them to make better use of the health services and to demand better standards of care. This has been strikingly illustrated in the field of family planning. Responsible parents, and these constitute the vast majority, limit the size of their family in the interests of the children themselves because they know that good education, housing and food are expensive. Our experience in a long term study of a representative sample of Aberdeen women having a first baby is that 10-15 years later more than 25% of all subsequent children have been unplanned and mostly unwanted. This occurred despite the fact that contraceptive advice has been available in Aberdeen as part of postnatal care since 1946. Most of those who attended came from social classes 1 and 2, the non-manual social groups, and very few from the semi- and unskilled groups. The introduction of the contraceptive pill transformed the situation and quickly replaced the vaginal diaphragm and coitus interruptus. Oral contraception began to be used in Aberdeen in 1964, and by 1967 the number of third and fourth births had fallen by 17 and 23% respectively. This occurred because the woman now had a reliable method of prevention which was under her own control. Wives are no longer dependent upon the husband taking the necessary precautions. It cannot have escaped notice that while there is now willingness on the part of the authorities to provide contraceptive advice on 'medical' grounds, there has been some resistance to giving it on 'social' grounds. This indicates a failure to recognise that family planning is a necessary prescription for responsible parenthood. The unplanned pregnancy in a healthy woman can cause serious deterioration in both physical and mental health, and may in some cases have an effect on the emotional health of the child if the mother herself has not been able to accept the situation. Contraceptive advice is therefore a part of good preventive medicine and should be freely available in the National Health Service.

Some mothers who have a strong desire to give each child the maximum opportunity for a good life may also wish to return to the work for which they have been trained. Indeed because the marriage rate is now so high it is very much in the national interest that women should be encouraged to return to work. In these circumstances it is scarcely surprising that when plans go wrong and an unplanned pregnancy does occur the emotional disturbance may be very intense. In the years 1938-47, 64% of all pregnancies terminated in Aberdeen were in those who had already had seven or more children. The indications were severe debility and exhaustion associated with excessive childbearing. Today emotional stress is much more important and only 10% of terminations were done because of excessive childbearing. In 1961-63 termination of pregnancy followed by sterilisation was performed almost equally in all social classes although classes 4 and 5 were over-represented slightly. On the other hand tubal ligation alone was performed much more frequently in social classes 4 and 5, especially 5, the semi- or unskilled occupational group. In fact it was used as a method of contraception in those who had shown that they were unable to prevent pregnancy by any other method. A study of the children of such women at the ages of 7+ and 9+ showed that in attainment tests at school they had scores which were much lower than those of the children of women from the same social class who were not sterilised because the mothers gave the impression that they could themselves prevent further pregnancy by using successfully one of the accepted methods of contraception. From 1957 onwards the fertility rate in Aberdeen has been much lower than that of Glasgow and Edinburgh. This is probably the result of the greater availability of advice and help in the prevention of unwanted pregnancies in Aberdeen. It represents a combined effort on the part of the hospital service, the local health authority and the family doctors.

A new problem is the rise in the illegitimacy rate especially in single women since 1955. In the past the rate was higher in Scotland than in England. In England the rate started to rise in 1955 whereas in Scotland this did not occur till 1958 by which time the English rate was much higher than the Scottish rate. In both countries the increase has been greatest in the upper social classes although the actual rate is still much higher in the lower social classes. In the past illegitimacy was more prevalent in the rural than in urban areas. The present increase shows the reverse trend because it started in London and the other large cities in the South of England and spread northwards and from the urban to the rural areas. In the past the most commonly associated causes have been poverty, lack of education and of security in the home. This picture does not fit the present situation. As Illsley and Gill have written: 'More value is now placed upon overt sexuality in the married as well as in the unmarried. If there is more extramarital sexuality need there be more extramarital pregnancy? Society wishes to prevent unintended conceptions by the most efficient means but it fears the emergence of a generation which does not cherish chastity. Until society decides for itself the moral behaviour which it regards as acceptable, there is no clear guidance for the individual. If an unwanted pregnancy does occur what are the current pressures which decide whether it will end in marriage, illegitimacy or abortion?'

Meanwhile a formidable and immediate problem has been raised for the gynaecologist who feels that, while termination of the pregnancy is not the cure of the problem, it may be the best for some individuals. The divorce rate and the illegitimacy rate amongst married women have increased in recent years. It has been the experience in the past that the break up of marriage is most common in those who marry young but whether this will be so today when so many in all social classes marry at an early age is not yet known. The rise in illegitimacy is not confined to Britain—it has occurred in most industrialised societies in Europe, America and Asia. We seem to be in a transition between the older sexual-marital pattern and a new code based on premarital sexual experience, experimentation based upon effective contraception and abortion in the last resort. During the transition many individuals suffer the penalties that still survive from a more clear-cut moral code. We know little about the late effects of illegitimate pregnancy in the young whatever the outcome. The increasing attention now being paid to the study of man in his environment by the universities, especially the increase in medico-social research, and the improved quality of the component of radio and television devoted to education is encouraging.

It is difficult to predict future trends in the birth rate. It is true that early marriage has the effect that most wives are at the height of their fertility and that fewer will be infertile, but there is no evidence that the young are having large families. In fact, if the first two children are of different sex, there is a strong possibility that there will be no more. There is no clear case for a government policy on population other than the provision of the best advice on contraception to those who desire it and to those who need it. No doubt fiscal policy could influence the birth rate indirectly but this would be only a marginal effect. What is most important is the provision of the means for improving the quality of life for those who are born; for example, the provision of day nurseries and nursery schools of high quality, crèches at places of work or the separate assessment of the income of husband and wife for tax purposes. Advice on the possible risks of foetal abnormality in any future pregnancy should be available and the diagnosis early in pregnancy of the presence of serious malformation would provide the opportunity for termination of the pregnancy and thus reduce the number of seriously handicapped children.

It is clear that we can define what could be called a 6th social class characterised by prenuptial conception or illegitimacy, unskilled manual occupation, unemployment, short stature, large numbers of children, high perinatal mortality rates especially associated with prematurity and malformations and a high incidence of mild mental subnormality amongst the children. Without interfering in any way with the parents' freedom of choice of family size the number of children in such families can be greatly reduced if the parents have easy access to sympathetic help and advice. Experience shows that few of these couples really wish to have more than three or four children. A reduction of family size in this way has great immediate advantages for both parents and children and also reduces the number of delinquent and problem children in the community.

FURTHER READING

B.B.C. *Morals and medicine*. Five discussions from the Third Programme. British Broadcasting Corporation, London.

Illsey, R. and Gill, D., 1968. New fashions in illegitimacy. *New Society*, 709. Nov. 14th.

Lorraine, J. A., 1970. *Sex and the population crisis.* William Heinemann Medical Books Ltd., London.

National Birthday Trust Fund, 1969. *Perinatal problems.* Butler, N. R. and Alberman, E. D. (eds.). Second report of the 1958 British Perinatal Mortality Survey. E. & S. Livingstone, Ltd., Edinburgh.

Orr, J. B., 1937. *Food, health and income.* Macmillan and Co. Ltd., London.

Platt, R. and Parkes, A. S. (eds.), 1967. *Social and genetic influences on life and death.* Oliver and Boyd, Edinburgh.

Titmuss, R. M., 1943. *Birth, poverty and wealth.* Hamish Hamilton Medical Books, London.

The author wishes to acknowledge that the work on which his paper depends was done during his tenure of a Belding Scholarship from the Association for Aid of Crippled Children, New York, U.S.A.

W. FERGUSON ANDERSON

Affluence and the elderly

It is a trite saying but indeed a true one that old age is not so bad when you consider the alternative. Although the length of life anticipated by a newly born baby is much longer than at the turn of the century, people of advanced years are not living much longer. In fact Bourlière[1] has drawn attention to the fact that in France the expectation of life of an individual of 80 years had fallen between 1805 and 1955. In 1805 a person who reached 80 years of age was indeed a 'tough chicken' and had almost certainly survived typhoid fever, typhus and perhaps smallpox; thus only the very fit survived at that time. In today's world many people not so fit reach old age.

Nevertheless there has been some increase now in the expectation of life of the elderly citizen. The figures for people aged 65 years in England and Wales in 1960 were for males 12·0 years and for females 15·2 years—and those compared with 11·3 years and 13·1 years respectively in 1930.

It is not easy to interpret this increased longevity in terms of prolonged activity, i.e., in the quality of survival. Affluence, by providing adequate nursing and medical attention, is possibly one factor ensuring that people who arrive in this age group are more frail and feeble than a century ago. While there are today many more old people than ever before, the greatest change is in their state of health. If present trends continue there will be more women over 75 years of an increasingly weakly type, preserved from death by their sex and their doctors. In 1967 in England and Wales there were 206,000 men between 80 and 84 years of age and 441,000 women. In 1981 corresponding figures are expected to be 247,000 and 560,000. Those 75 years and over in England and Wales will increase from 2,131,000 in 1966 to 2,725,000 in 1981, an increase of nearly one-third. The Russians Chebotarev and Sachuk[3] revealed the comparison between the sexes in their study of 27,181 people over 80 years

101

of age in the Ukraine (Table I). They found nearly seven times
as many women over 100 years as men, and the mortality
figures from any geriatric unit will confirm the near immor-
tality of the aged female.

TABLE I

| | A | B | | C |
	80-90	90 *and over*	100 *and over*	*Total* 80 *and over*
Men	5,899	1,734	52	7,633
Women	13,526	6,022	363	19,548
Both sexes	19,425	7,756	415	27,181

Please note that the 100 and over in the Table are
taken as an isolated group (A+B=C)

The old men are a group with an excess suicide risk, with
physical illness the commonest precipitating factor, but both
sexes in old age show in this modern age an ever increasing
admission rate to mental hospitals. Between 1951 and 1960
mental hospital first admission rate for elderly men increased
by between 30 and 40% and for elderly women by just over
40%. Munch-Petersen[5] discussing problems relating to patients
with senile dementia stated that 1·4% or approximately 1,300
elderly people in Copenhagen suffered from senile dementia
and this number will probably have increased to about 1,700
in 1980.

Older people are at risk from physical disease, mental illness
and social problems. There are few who would deny the need
for preventive measures to overcome, among other factors, the
evils of the new megapolis concept of living. There is need to
separate the two great sciences of gerontology and geriatric
medicine. Gerontology is concerned with the study of the
process of 'normal' ageing in animals or in man whereas
geriatric medicine is the subdivision of medicine involved in the
problems of ageing with superimposed disease.

Examination of the individual from 55 years and upwards
shows certain common points. Physical health is frequently

neglected because symptoms of minor nature which occur are attributed to ageing and not to disease. Williamson[8] in his survey of people over 65 years in three general practices found much unreported illness, i.e. complaints which the individual had but had not bothered to tell to his doctor, so that these troubles were unknown to anyone. Such unreported illnesses included incontinence of urine, locomotor disability, foot trouble, anaemia and dementia. On the other hand, breathlessness, swelling of ankles and paralysis of limbs if these occurred were recognised as disease.

Accurate diagnosis, important in younger age groups, is even more essential in the elderly because of failing homeostatic mechanisms and is improving with the realisation that multiple pathology is the rule and not the exception. Older people are still labelled as senile and Pritchard and Kelly[7] analysed 98 cases referred to a geriatric unit with the diagnosis of 'senility'. Two-thirds of the patients were over 80 and in addition to the label 'senile' a wide distribution of diagnoses was made. Some 34 patients were found with 'senile' only as their diagnosis and from information available it was shown that the popular connotation of senility was built up because of the general impairment of physique, special senses and lack of social self-confidence. Seventy-two (75·5%) of patients referred were admitted and 230 diagnoses were made in these patients, i.e. 3·19 lesions per patient. Some 23 of the 72 patients admitted were discharged home, nine to eventide homes and seven remained as inpatients. Twenty-five died, and others were mainly referred to other hospitals. Eventually nearly 50% left hospital. The authors concluded 'We eschew the term "senility", preferring to rely on the honoured methods of clinical investigation. We believe that one is ill not because one is old but because there is something wrong. We also believe that the image of senility has stolen symptoms referable to disease and applied them indiscriminately to both the normal changes of senescence and to the abnormal changes of degenerative pathology conditions.' A plea is made for thorough assessment of the apparently senile elderly person and that the word 'senile' in isolation as a diagnosis be dropped. The question must be asked when did it become relatively unimportant in medical practice to make a diagnosis in the old. Is this a symptom of the affluent society when the young and middle-aged are regarded as the important and productive members of society?

A very common cause of ill health in the West of Scotland is obesity; this may be due to the local dietetic habits of the people. Using a nomogram which by measuring height and weight gives a percentage overweight it was found that blood pressure begins to rise and the cardiac silhouette increases at around 25% overweight. These measurements were taken in women because in our series at the Rutherglen Consultative Health Centre one hundred and eleven fit fat women were found but not a single healthy fat man was discovered. Obesity may well be associated with mental ill health and in our series the common causes of emotional upset in older people were as follows: living alone, worry about physical health or the health of a loved one, bereavement and, in men, compulsory retirement.

In the pattern of modern society around 32% of people over 65 years of age live alone and many do not like it. For single or widowed women the figure rises to 50% and approximately 26% of people over 65 have no living relatives. In an excellent debate in the House of Lords on March 23rd, 1955, Viscount Soulbury having recalled Beveridge's giants in the way of progress—disease, idleness, ignorance, squalor and want—added a sixth, loneliness. These giants stand astride the path of progress of the elderly citizen and in this debate Soulbury quoted a letter found after the death of Robert Louis Stevenson which stated 'desiderata—health, two to three hundred per year and Oh, du liebe Gott, Friends'.

Loneliness, seldom seen in the bad old Glasgow tenement, seems a mark of middle-classness, almost of respectability, and perhaps of moderate affluence. In a survey of the over 80's in Stockport, Brockington and Lempert,[2] found that 3·9% were never visited, 6·5% had no relatives visiting and 15·1% were never visited by friends. Loneliness is surely a remediable disease which would be abolished by careful planning and the help of voluntary workers. Here is the chance for the health centre with its team of doctors, social workers, nurses, chiropodists and perhaps physiotherapists. The need exists to forge links between the patient's home and the all-day club, between hospital and day hospital to ensure by one way or another ascertainment of the lonely and their continuing supervision. This supervision should include adequate nutrition, remedial exercises, provision of interests and the encouragement to stop looking in at oneself and to start thinking of others older and weaker than oneself. Loneliness, like hypothermia, is more common in the modern new building of today and our cities must be broken down into smaller communities, e.g. of 20,000 to 30,000. The older citizen becomes lost in the large town.

Physical examination at certain periods of life, e.g. 55 years of age or following retirement or bereavement, would do much to improve the mental health of older people. At least such a procedure would make them familiar with the facilities available to them should need arise. If this was considered impracticable a start could be made in a much more restricted way. If a general practitioner with a list of 2,000 people examined each individual who became 65 years of age in the preceding year he would have to examine 16 people per year. In the 17 years' work at the Rutherglen Consultative Health Centre the improvement in the mental health of older people following a physical examination never fails to impress.

Bereavement is a time not only of mental ill health but of risk of death for the survivor and care must be taken that the older person is not lost sight of and, after an appropriate interval, is encouraged to mix again with colleagues and friends. The possession of a sound religious faith is of great value to the individual.

Compulsory retirement—a man made idle—presents no problem if he is well educated. Such an individual often finds himself busier than ever. But even in this group there are exceptions and preparation for retirement now seems the correct approach. Since 1959, the Glasgow Retirement Council has provided pre-retirement training courses and hobbies and crafts centres for those who have retired and has encouraged part-time re-employment and the formation of retired employees' associations.

In this field it would seem essential for any government to have knowledge of the labour force required in the next 25 years or so, in view of increasing automation, so that the work available may be shared and retraining programmes for part-time employment instituted at around 55 years of age. The total working life may require to be extended but the actual working hours per week greatly reduced. A place must be found in the community of tomorrow for the knowledge, ability and skill of the older worker to avoid the loss of status caused by earlier and earlier compulsory retirement.

The social problems of the elderly abound—financially in 1965 22·7% of married couples retired had an income of £10 to £12 10s. per week, 22·3% of single men had £5-£6 per week and 42·1% of single women £4-£5 per week. In our survey work it is surprising that old people do not mention finance as a first cause of difficulty.

There is much evidence, however, of unmet social need, for example in the provision of home helps, and but for the help of relatives, neighbours and friends, the welfare and hospital services could not cope for one day. Outside hospitals and institutions there are more than three times as many old persons with severe incapacity or bedfast.

Encouragement and supply of supporting social service must be given outwith hospitals and homes as even the slightest alteration in trend would swamp our inpatient resources. Every assistance should be given to relatives to enable them to help older relatives. At present in the United Kingdom 42% of those over 67 years of age live with their children, in the United States of America 28%, Denmark 20% and Sweden less than 10%. Is this the pattern of affluence?

In contrast there is no difficulty in discharging elderly patients from hospitals in U.S.S.R. They are required immediately as baby-sitters to let the married woman return to work.

In Eastern countries, for example in Singapore, there seems little incontinence in long-stay wards—there the elderly are thin, mobile and perhaps have fewer emotional problems. There seem to be in our civilisation the problems of rejection and ever increasing depression among the elderly. Newman[6] feels that a man's behaviour patterns can be reversed by imposing intolerable strains on a normally functioning brain. He considers that the experience of prisoners of war subjected to such strains provides a plausible theory of incontinence. Under certain conditions the prisoner of war becomes indifferent to his surroundings—apathetic, dishevelled and incontinent.

Newman compares this description with the condition of many old people, especially in institutions, but also in society when they are subjected as they often are to isolation, privation and humiliation. An understanding of their needs might reduce the dimensions of the problem of incontinence.

There is one cheering note in today's world: Walter McKain[4] has written about retirement marriage. This is a new phenomenon typified by a question sent for urgent advice:

'Is there any state near Iowa where a couple can go to be married in a hurry? We would like to get married as soon as possible as his children want to put him in a rest home.

Sarah'

This book on retirement marriages is the recording of the experience of 100 older couples who married when the bride was at least 60 and the groom 65 years of age or older and only those marriages in which both partners had been married previously are reported. Among the factors which formed the basis for a successful retirement marriage were that the brides and grooms should know each other well before marrying and that the marriage should be approved by children and friends. Some individuals, according to McKain, are so constituted that they will be happy in almost any marriage situation while others do not have the capacity for a successful marriage. If the bride and groom are satisfied with their lives up to this point and do not feel that luck has been against them they have a good chance of marital success.

The future then presents us with more frail old women, increasing admission rates among the elderly to mental hospitals, and urgent need for ascertainment of the 'at risk' groups for correct diagnosis and appropriate early therapy. Nutritional advice is essential with abolition of obesity and efforts made to maintain the mental health of the elderly in the face of worry about physical health, bereavement, loneliness and retirement. Planning is necessary to make the best use of the total labour force in the most appropriate way. Unmet social needs must be met with the endeavour to support to the full all who help the ill elderly person at home. Retirement marriage offers one happy solution. Problems of the elderly are eminently soluble provided thought and money is devoted to their solution.

108 THE BIOLOGY OF AFFLUENCE

1. Bourlière, T., 1963. Methods of measuring biological age in man. *Health protection of the elderly*, WHO Seminar Working Paper Euro 245/2. WHO Regional Office for Europe, Copenhagen.
2. Brockington, F. and Lempert, S. M. 1966. *The social needs of the over eighties*. Manchester University Press, Manchester.
3. Chebotarev, D. F. and Sachuk, N., 1964. Sociomedical examination of longevous people in the U.S.S.R. *Amer. J. Geront.*, 19, 435.
4. McKain, W. C., 1968. *Retirement marriage*. University of Connecticut, Storrs, Connecticut.
5. Munch-Petersen, S., 1966. Problems relating to patients with senile dementia. *Acta. psychiat. Scandinav.*, Suppl. 191, 42, 99.
6. Newman, J. L., 1969. The prevention of incontinence. *Proceedings of 8th International Congress of Gerontology*, 2, 75.
7. Pritchard, J. G. and Kelly, J. C. C., 1967. The image of senility. *J. Roy. Coll. Gen. Practit.*, 14, 50.
8. Williamson, J., 1966. Ageing in modern society. *Paper presented to Royal Society of Health*, Edinburgh, Nov. 9th.

FURTHER READING

Anderson, W. F., 1971. *Practical management of the elderly*. Blackwell Scientific Publications, Oxford.

The world setting

THE HUMAN SITUATION

Man's reason, individual and collective, must solve the problem of the penalties of affluence just as he tries to solve the tragedies of poverty. By trying to shelter himself from the cradle to the grave from an inclement environment, from war, famine and pestilence, and by buffering himself so far as he can from the outrages of cruel misfortune man now minimises the survival value of many of the genetic characteristics with which, to varying extent, members of the human family are endowed. What is the penalty? Overpopulation obviously: is too much expected of the surviving weak? Is there more maladjustment and intolerance in consequence? Does man, indeed, carry a large number of inactive or 'non-sense' genes as some would have us believe, to provide a reserve of unused capacity to continue his evolution should the right conditions occur for their exploitation?[15]

Malthus[14] thought that science could overcome the increasing disparity between world food supply and world population. Indeed, he did not doubt that an answer would be forthcoming, but some of his successors have. We need to determine how far progress is being achieved and how to overcome the problems facing agriculture, the storage and transport of food, air pollution, ischaemic heart disease, the elderly, and some of the penalties of increasing sophistication of food in an affluent community. There must be a will on our part, to see that the anachronism of vast populations leading lives steeped in poverty and ill health disappears in a world where the affluent are worried about the penalties of access to materials and facilities in excess of those adequate for their physiological and psychological health. Man already has a thousand secrets for mastering nature, for increasing productivity, for prolonging

life, for liquidating want, but he seems unable to educate his
fellow man so that these be not only made known but practised
with intelligence. Likewise, he seems unable to appreciate the
basic principles which provide for a *mens sana in corpore sano* and
that for some *mens sana* may also be a *mens creatrix*. The description of the bursts of strenuous weekly exercise which some
Scandinavian business executives have to take part in does not
reflect sound physiological and medical principles.

In rescuing people from unhealthy hovels and giving them
homes with baths and bedrooms, the emphasis in this country
has been on houses and more houses. Other facilities—shops,
cinemas, cafés, community centres, playgrounds, inns and
pubs, places to kick a ball around—all these should be provided
at the same time. The tragedy of Easterhouse in Glasgow is that
a collection of houses was built and not a community. 'Well
intentioned civic power created a morass of boredom, a multi-
tude of idle hands with nothing constructive to do. Beehives
full of people with nowhere to go.'

Modern man wants wider spaces: playing fields, golf courses,
football fields, tennis courts. As such spaces occupy areas
where wheat or animals could grow, will this be declared anti-
social in this land of ours, where we have a greater concentration
of persons to the square mile than has India? Every ten years
we lose to non-agricultural uses an area of land about the size of
a county like Lanarkshire or Nottinghamshire. Man also wants
to see a little of unspoilt Nature. In part, this has been achieved
through provision of national parks. We still see people looking
for archaic types of adventure and being frequently frustrated
in their pursuit. It is here that the Highlands and Islands
provide the space and the setting. Atrophy of the spirit and
creative capacity as well as the capacity to enjoy life simply,
can stealthily creep upon us unless we take care to cultivate
their outlet.

Growth

Children in our affluent and developing societies are growing
progressively faster and the difference in final stature between
the social classes in the affluent countries is diminishing.
Puberty has been occurring progressively earlier. The period of
adolescence is, apart from childbearing, the most eventful

period of life physically, biologically and emotionally in this affluent world.

Adolescence is the age of self consciousness and sex consciousness. Anxiety may lead to disturbances of appetite and possibly of digestion. The adolescent in our Western democracies is probably at a greater disadvantage than in more authoritarian and primitive regimes where the emergence into adulthood is accepted with greater demonstration.

The increasing age gap, resulting from the trend to earlier growth-spurt, and the increasing mean age of the adult population tend to enhance disparity in outlook between youth and adult. As older people have become more tolerant of these 'teenagers' and their problems a greater sympathy is abroad, but now there follows the consequence of abuse of this permissive tolerance.

Differences in the timing, nature and extent of the adolescent growth-spurt and other pubertal changes will be reflected in different nutrient requirements. With improvement of the environment of which food is a part the secular trend has been towards earlier emergence of adolescence and until recently the evidence indicated that it was becoming more intense. There is some evidence that the rate is now diminishing.

The biological advantages of childbearing in late adolescence are generally offset by the difficult social circumstance and the poor environment that so frequently surround it. Inadequate nutrition, leading to subnormal growth and impaired health, together with poor education, play an adverse part in young primigravidae. Marriage of the under-20 bride is twice as likely to fail as is that of older age groups.

The taller a woman is, the more effective her reproductive efficiency, her lactational performance and the percentage of fat in that milk.[2, 5, 9, 10]

Obesity

Moderate adiposity was admired in our earlier civilisations as an indication of health, beauty and affluence. In the present century there has been increased interest in obesity, its potential health hazards, prevention and treatment. Obesity is no longer fashionable but a threat to a full and long life. The incidence of the overweight is held to increase up to about the age of 40 in men and 50 in women. The trap is that with increasing mechanisation there is reduced energy expenditure in many occupational and many recreational pursuits.

A recent comparison of the major arteries in 22,509 autopsies from 15 cities of the world revealed variations in degree of atherosclerosis which could be best explained by environmental rather than racial differences. The most important environmental factor studied was dietary fat. As almost all people studied had some degree of disease present, the increase in severity with age was presumably aggravated, rather than induced, by these environmental factors. The only outstanding exceptions were the Asian Indians in South Africa, who showed surprisingly severe disease. It was suggested that this might relate to the high incidence of diabetes mellitus. It was concluded that there was no obvious association between extent of atherosclerotic fatty streaks or raised lesions in either the coronary arteries or the aorta, and obesity. Nevertheless, the well-known relationship between obesity and cardiovascular death rates cannot be denied on the basis of these data because obesity does increase the likelihood of sudden death and the ease of developing angina pectoris with increased work of the heart. Below a certain 'threshold' of atherosclerotic disease, such aggravating factors as hypertension, diabetes, and by inference hyperlipaemia, might not necessarily affect the arterial lesion to the degree of severity required for clinical disease to be observed.[12]

As Dr R. L. Richards has pointed out in an earlier chapter, the evidence of an association of increasing obesity and the stresses of life with rising death rate from coronary heart disease is still inconclusive.

Family and social life

Affluent man wants at least one car per family with garage, parking places and a little free room between bumper and bumper. He is increasingly frustrated by constraints to his motoring. However, he may be driven to walk, which would be a very good thing. Meantime, he is afraid to walk to the pillar box to post a letter because he may be thought to be failing in business. If he takes his car he may lose the parking place near his house. In London this may cost him £25 per annum or more.

The indulgences which are open in the state of affluence are many but because of this and the spread of choice open to him Man is frequently in a dilemma about his behaviour, actions and reactions and sometimes he longs for a constraint from without, which will save him worrying, or for someone to whom he may turn. The Church, the authoritarian father or civil authority or State, can to some extent act wisely in this respect. Military service had, at least, this advantage that it provided a sheltered fallow period to allow young men to adjust themselves to adulthood and responsibility.

On the other hand we must note that the peculiar pattern of upbringing and authoritarian family relations in India prevent Indian youths becoming independent. There are distinct traces of a dependency pattern which definitely thwarts autonomy and the attainment of self-sufficiency. This attitude cripples civil servants in arriving at decisions.

The caste system is an all-pervading feature of the social structure in India so that it has ramifications for the entire action, behaviour, relationships, etc., of the people. The ascriptive basis of the caste system completely thwarts the process of autonomy, character formation and self-sufficiency.

The attitude towards the State and the polity may tend to be one of the relationship between a benevolent patriarch and his subjects. The people look up to the State for all their needs, difficulties and problems, without making any effort to solve some of these on their own.

Family, kin, caste, age grades, polity, economy, etc., thus frequently put a premium on a dependency pattern on the elders in an emerging country. There may be a great deal of imposition by the elders on the youngsters. The decision taken by an individual is thus largely dictated by the decision of the kin group.

Affluence if unwisely controlled leads through its very superabundance, to stagnation, to early clotting of blood vessels, in heart and brain, as well as of roads. The affluent society generally sets the pattern, the glossy magazine and TV see that the Joneses are well informed. Even if this is economically not a sound model, nevertheless, the less affluent striving to emulate may benefit, as for example, by consuming a better diet. Indeed, those who have tried to introduce new foods to compensate for the deficiencies of an area seldom succeed unless the affluent are also seen to consume them. Sophistication in food brings quality control although frequently there is some damage in processing requiring compensation.

Much of the rebellion of our youth today is against the state of mind produced by affluence. Gandhi rebelled against this and tried to produce a state of contentment with things largely as they are and with everyone doing something worthwhile in the country. This philosophy has not yielded much fruit for his people. He has failed meantime. They now demand higher standards of social wellbeing.

Serenity without affluence has been achieved in some populations. For example, there is a small kingdom in the Himalayas, Hunza, where there are descendants of three deserters from the army of Alexander the Great who settled there with Persian wives. According to Noel Barker[3] they have had no wars for 2,000 years. They have no money, no crime, no diseases, and they rarely die before 90 years. They keep their numbers limited without contraception and without abortion.

Economics and planning

In the U.K. an affluent society has emerged since 1951 in the form of a modified capitalism, under successive Conservative governments and continued in a more modified form under Labour. Between them Sidney Webb and David Lloyd George laid the foundation of the British Welfare State and Beveridge, at Churchill's instigation, provided the pattern in 1942. F. D. Roosevelt and his Brains Trust formed a similar symbiotic team in the U.S.A. The U.S.A. stands out as one of the models of the new managed capitalism. Its planning, programming budgeting system (P.P.B.S.) applied to all Federal civil agencies could be a guide to us on the quality of the supporting detailed analysis of specific programmes needed, particularly at geographically decentralised key points. Post-war affluent societies still show grave imperfections, particularly of a 'stop-go' character, of injustices to whole social groups, of imbalance between private and public sectors.

In Western democracy, life is far freer and more comfortable for far more citizens than ever before in the history of the human race. Life has a new dignity. The conscience of the affluent is increasingly distressed by hunger and ill-treatment.

Given a choice, a majority will opt for this capitalist way of life. Judged in terms of that individualistic pursuit of happiness which the American founding fathers laid down as the aim of the republic, Communism is still an inferior way of life compared to that of the affluent societies of the West. As R. H. Crossman[4] has pointed out, this does not alter the fact that, in terms of military power, of industrial development, of technological advance, of mass literacy, and eventually of mass consumption too, the planned socialist economy is proving its capacity to outpace and overtake the wealthy and comfortable economies. The lead is being narrowed by the economic use of resources under a planned economy in the East and by the wastefulness of the artificially induced obsolescence of personal belongings, which is a main motive force of the affluent consuming West.

Racial factors in success

Lord Snow, some months ago, was discussing why it was that Jews had been so remarkably successful. In his speech he indicated that genetic inheritance is far more important than environment or good fortune in establishing a man's ability to achieve. There are evidences, he believed, of distinctive differences between ethnic and racial groups which can be categorised in terms of a 'gene pool'. Study of these he believed might repay the effort. Whether we shall ever be able to identify genetic characters to select potential mathematicians, musicians or athletes is for the future, but on the other hand are we foolish in behaving as if everyone must be given the benefit of the doubt? We do know that certain long-legged African tribes make good jumpers and here inheritance must obviously play a part. Snow suggests that everyone should be treated as being able to achieve 10% more than they are actually capable of, but society should be careful of giving extended education to everyone in the higher realms of mathematics, music, athletics or other specialist fields. 'The idea that every American could become President of the U.S.A. was true but stupid' he is reported to have said. It was liable to upset a lot of people who liked to believe that their fate was in their own hands and that given good fortune, which they inevitably did not profess to have, they could compose a symphony, paint great pictures, write great books and in their spare moments be film stars. But the world requires a broad spectrum of human capacity and performance from most of us.

Denis Gabor[7] suggests 'it is probable or, at least, possible that a significant step towards a stationary population and towards eugenics could be achieved by a single change in the Budget: increase the allowances and subsidies for the first and second child, but cut them off completely for the third child, except in the case of couples who can give proof of good heredity'. But there is the rub! If something like one third of the parents were allowed to qualify for this a reproductive rate just sufficient for a stationary population could be established with a minimum of hardship. Everything beyond this he would leave on a voluntary basis. Advice bureaux would be provided to help those with hereditary diseases to abstain from having children. Such are the views of some who have given thought to the matter; others consider this would have no effect on fecundity.[6] Let us remind ourselves that Hitler also gave thought to the population and racial problems of the Third Reich! It is frequently forgotten by those concerned in advising on population control of developing peoples that the old and sick are dependent on having sufficient male children surviving that their old age and future welfare is taken care of. Until the time when such security is provided by civic or governmental action there will continue to be the need for large numbers of male children. Official projections for the U.K. by the Registrar General put the population at 66 millions by the end of the century and not at 75 millions as formerly thought.

The application of science and technology to development

The attitude of reverence for Nature in some countries, for example India, militates by and large against rational manipulation of the forces of Nature. Active orientation towards life and reality rather than a ready or fatalistic acceptance is very necessary to exploit the forces of Nature. A frame of mind must be engendered which sustains a continuous enquiry into those forces pertaining to both Nature and society which need to be harnessed, modified, manipulated and changed for the benefit of Man. Communism may take advantage of such a change.

At the inter-governmental conference on the Application of Science and Technology to the Development of Asia

(CASTASIA) organised by UNESCO in co-operation with the United Nations Economic Commission for Asia and the Far East which took place in New Delhi recently, the Director-General, M. René Maheu, pointed out that the gap separating the affluent countries from the poor countries is steadily widening because the economic advances are rapidly offset by the rising populations. There must be, he observed, planning of the population growth, through better use of the human and material resources. Science and technology must cease to be imported magic in need of constant renewal: they must strike root in the social and cultural realities so that they may grow and flourish as local plants. Strong motivation, determination and direction are required on the part of the governments. There must be full use of mass communication techniques, functional literacy programmes, science clubs and fairs, co-operation with national and international organisations—both governmental and non-governmental—including women's organisations, and with special emphasis on reaching the rural population.

In pursuit of the fruits of affluence, and heady with the immediate success of our human activities in exploitation of natural resources, we have been somewhat insensitive to the consequences of deterioration of some of our terrestrial and aquatic environments, changes in water balance, loss of plant and animal species, pollution of the atmosphere, eutrophication of our inland waters, all as the result of the tremendous expansion of these human activities, including population growth. Unless we take appropriate action at national, regional and international level these may become irreversible and produce a critical situation that could seriously harm the present and future of mankind. But we are well served in this country by advisory committees of scientists who are continuously looking at these things. UNESCO, on the basis of the success of the International Biological Programme, has decided that its interest in the Biosphere will continue, and through using non-governmental organisations to the full, the post-I.B.P. Programme will be inter-governmental and concerned with man and the Biosphere. I.C.S.U. in September 1968 appointed an *ad hoc* committee on 'Man-made changes to the Environment' and the symposium organised jointly by I.U.B.S. and I.B.P. on

E

September 29/30, 1969, at the Royal Society was the sounding board on this subject.

Even the general problem of the biological contamination of the planets has been considered by the International Committee on Space Research (COSPAR). As Sir Bernard Lovell[11] points out investigation, itself, inevitably carries a risk of contamination.

Agriculture

Looking round we note that spectacular results can be achieved where education is sound. Irrigation, modern inputs, and farmer training have raised Israel's food production by 150% in a decade. Countries like Mexico, Taiwan, Thailand and the Philippines have increased their food production faster than their population sizes. Through new wheats and rice (IR8) FAO can now report that in the Far East—the world's major deficit area—food production increased by 5% despite bad weather in many parts. Japan has become affluent through a sound economic development which enables them to produce commercially and import the food they will require. Her agriculture is very intense, like that of the Dutch though quite different in character. On the other hand, where agricultural resources are extensive and at least potentially rich, as in the Indian sub-continent and many of the African, Latin American, and South-East Asian countries, agriculture should be given a very high emphasis in any development programme.

The Aid-giving affluent countries must place higher emphasis on assistance in the area of food production and on food commodity aid as an interim measure where necessary to prevent serious hunger.

There are those who advocate that the best way to meet food supply problems in the developing countries might be to put back into production all the acres that the U.S.A. has taken out of production because of surplus production. In effect, the idea is that because the U.S.A. is efficient in agriculture, it should produce much of the food that is needed around the world and make it available on an Aid basis in so far as that is necessary. That conclusion has been examined and rejected, though the need for temporary shipments of food supplies from the U.S.A. will continue, but these shipments on a non-commercial basis will not remain a permanent part of their policy. In any case, the annual surplus of wheat in the U.S.A. is only about 1% of present total grain production.

Many countries cannot yet effectively absorb much capital for agricultural development at the present time. To take irrigation as an example, there are many irrigation projects around the developing world which are not giving reasonable yields or not leading to significant intensification of production. If proper advantage is to be taken of irrigation, for instance by the introduction of multiple cropping, extensive changes have to be effected in farming practices, including the proper selection of seeds and the proper performance of field work through mechanisation, application of fertilisers, use of pesticides, efficient marketing and adequate credit. In other words, the provision of technical advice, becomes the limiting factor, rather than any shortage of capital. If these problems can be solved, large and sometimes spectacular results can be achieved.

The way farmers are prepared to welcome new varieties of wheat, rice and maize is encouraging. Man's technological ingenuity in developing new ways of feeding an expanding population is beyond doubt; much less sure is his political maturity in ensuring that the benefits are reasonably distributed.

The suggestion has been made that world-wide adoption of vegetarian diets is the solution to world wide caloric under-nutrition, since animal production is relatively inefficient in conversion. It would be inconceivable to expect countries of North America and Europe to reverse the tendency to increase the proportion of animal products in their diets as they have progressed from poverty to plenty.

In a symposium held a few years ago by the Rockefeller Foundation on 'The strategy for the conquest of hunger' its president, Dr George Harrar,[8] concluded that the consensus of opinion of the speakers was one of cautious but justifiable optimism. All were convinced that if governments, national planners, and investors paid proper attention to the modernisation of agriculture in the developing countries, it would be possible during the next few years to meet growing needs. Efficient programmes of agricultural modernisation will also stimulate industry, since improved production requires chemical fertilisers, pesticides, improved seed, machinery, irrigation and transport systems.

In the strategy for the conquest of hunger, Harrar pointed out that there seem to be six critical elements in a successful national effort to accelerate agricultural production:

(1) Each individual nation must establish production goals which are ambitious enough to merit enthusiastic participation by government, by industry, and by the farmer, and they must be technically and economically sound. They must be formulated co-operatively by knowledgeable economists, agricultural scientists, businessmen, and political leaders.

(2) Manpower and resources must be concentrated initially on rapid acceleration of production and profitability of the nation's most vital agricultural commodities—those which are produced on the greatest numbers of farms—and education of farmers.

(3) The technology of each commodity must be developed for, and tested in, the localities in which it is to be used. There must be recognition of the deplorable inadequacy of technology for improving food crops and major animal species, particularly for the tropics and for many of the arid regions of the world.

The tropics with their year-round growing temperatures represent the greatest underdeveloped source of food in the world today. It has been said that 'in a great wide ring around the globe, they are a potential food source which, through research, man can make into a veritable cornucopia'.

Dr C. P. McMeekan of New Zealand[13] until he retired recently was the Senior Agriculturist of the World Bank and responsible for setting up loan schemes to some 24 developing countries for increased animal production programmes—loan schemes expected to affect 21,000 farmers, 37 million acres of land, 6 million head of beef cattle, 100,000 head of dairy cattle and 250,000 head of sheep. He recently said of the future that there was still more usable land than used land and more poorly used land than land well used. In this he was quoting Dr Kellogg, one of the U.S.A.'s leading soil experts. In effect, well over half of the world's 8·7 billion acres of cultivatable land is lying idle and ignored by farmers and this does not include grazing lands. The existing used lands could treble their output in many areas, e.g. New Zealand and the United States of America. The world's population of six thousand millions which would be reached by the end of the century could be matched by a doubling of the output. To this end significant increase in population should cease and countries such as Africa and the lands of the Amazon and the River Plate should increase production immensely—particularly if Africa can be freed of animal disease.

McMeekan pointed out that shortage of capital is not a serious drawback. He has never found the Bank short of funds to lend for feasible projects. Unfortunately, too many farmers do not have the will to produce more than that necessary for their own survival. This lack of will and skill is the critical labour problem. Incentives and mobilisation of inputs are necessary. While the future cannot be predicted, futures can be invented. It is man's ability to invent which has made human society what it is.

If the yields are high on the experimental stations but in practice averages are low, scientific advances are 'on the shelf' so that for some reason the farmer is unable to make profitable use of them. Only for wheat and rice have determined efforts been made to create varieties with wide adaptation. Few of the root crops, the grain legumes, the cereal grains, the fruits and vegetables, or the major animal species have received sufficient attention in the tropical regions.

Dr Autret and his colleagues[1] have pointed out that where wheat, millet and sorghum are the staple foodstuffs, priority in research should be given to lysine-rich varieties rather than to high protein content as diets with these already have a satisfactory protein-calorie ratio.

For rice, priority in research is the other way round, that is on increasing protein content. The IR8 is a notable varietal advance.

Maize is in an intermediate position. A notable gain can only be achieved by developing varieties rich in lysine and tryptophan, as has been done for Opaque 2 variety. An increase in protein content is also desirable, and a greater ecological range.

For roots and tubers research should deal with an improvement of protein content and, in addition, in the case of cassava, with improvement in protein quality. However, diets based on roots and tubers have such a high protein deficit that their gradual replacement by cereals is recommended.

Great caution is needed in the implementation of programmes of enrichment by industrially prepared amino acids. When supplementation is necessary it must mostly be polyvalent. Natural protein supplements to the staple food must still form the major means of correction.

To continue with Dr Harrar's points:

(4) Nations must organise production campaigns sharply focused on important commodities. Governments must supply farms with the necessary agricultural chemicals, machinery, and credit when needed and at reasonable cost, perhaps through networks of service centres at which farmers may obtain their supplies with relative ease.

(5) Price policies must permit the farmer a reasonable profit. He who works and invests must share liberally in the gains or there will be none.

(6) Forward planning is essential to develop the national capability to produce, to transport, to store and to market the greater abundance and to provide through research an increasingly greater range of opportunities for diversification of the basic agricultural industry.

At a recent symposium in Nottingham University, Professor R. H. Tuck[17] of Reading University pointed out that a project must pay for itself if it is to be emulated. At the end of the day all major assistance must be paid for in one way or another. The choice of the original project should be such as to use inputs available and be integrated to these if possible. That means there must be a demand for the product. Money is not the real problem. 'Pay' in the above context means to offer acceptable other produce or services in exchange, and 'acceptable' in this context means to help with the running costs of the project. To remove the protein-calorie deficiency—the world's main problem—requires more than even that:

(1) Locality by locality current rates of appropriate production or free exchange commensurate with the needs of the population must rise. This emphasis on locality is because of difficulties of international transfer on concessional terms.

(2) Prospective rates of increase in production must be equal

to potential needs of population, the potential needs being those obtaining in a situation where mortality rates are in no way restricted by low income.

The crucial factors emerging from developing into developed nation-hood are:

(1) Birth rate. This is the essential determinant of the potential growth, assuming death rate is controlled.

(2) Possibility of increase in production capacity to match or provide for real needs for all.

An imbalance in these means descending standards for the poorer sections even though the average could be rising. The birth rate need not be stationary provided it is in balance, as will be seen from a study of the Hutterites.

Today's 15,000 Hutterites, a Protestant sect descended from 440 pioneers who emigrated to North America in the 1870's, are expected to number more than 55 million by the year 2168 if the present rate of growth continues. The unit of their society is the communal farm, which is worked by about 100 people. Every aspect of life and social organisation is determined by religious principles that have not changed much since the sixteenth century. Until now they have been extraordinarily successful in maintaining a mediaeval way of life set in a modern world. But the task of providing land and capital for their numerous descendants is becoming increasingly difficult, as they have possibly the highest birth rate in the world owing to their condemnation of birth control and their farming success. Generations of inbreeding have produced a superfecund strain of human species. 'Be fruitful and multiply' is a principal tenet. They have accepted modern medicine so infant mortality is low. The death rate is amongst the lowest in the world. The popula-tion is now doubling every 17 years. There are rigid taboos against teenage marriage and premarital sex. Their only other concession to the twentieth century is their acceptance of modern farming methods.

Hutterite colonies have none of the cultural amenities of modern societies; there is little intellectual stimulation and open affection between man and wife is discouraged. But the sense of belonging to a sacred community and the peace of mind that comes from acceptance of an undoubted creed are apparently powerful compensations.

In this people we have an unusual grouping of some of the components which go to make an affluent society and yet we would be unwilling to accept it as a model of an affluent society, for while it has kept personal indulgence within bounds in doing so the creative instinct seems to have been suppressed.

PESTICIDES AND OTHER TOXIC CHEMICALS

Pesticides continue to play an important role in the protection of agricultural and horticultural crops, livestocks and stored foods, particularly in the affluent countries. Without them farm productivity and the quality of food would fall appreciably. The search for alternatives to pesticides for crop and food protection, while yielding valuable information and indications of novel approaches, does not yet provide us with many economically practical alternatives of general application, but progress is being made.

The persistence of some compounds has led to their world-wide use and great concern has been expressed about those that are stable beyond the period for which they are required to be effective in practice. Residues of such compounds may remain over long periods, not only in the area in which they are used but in the environment as a whole. Fortunately their detection is made possible by very sensitive analytical techniques.

Because of the very great advantages, both to individuals and to the community, of some of these compounds in such fields as hygiene and public health, timber preservation, and the industrial moth-proofing of wool, no hasty restrictions should be placed on their non-agricultural uses unless there are reasonable grounds for believing there is a risk. But studies of the disposal of sludge or effluent and total quantities is urgently needed. Much further research is needed on the ecological and toxicological significance to wildlife of pesticide residues in the environment. The real hazards of even small scale use particularly to soil invertebrates and birds should be assessed before their application in this field. The accumulative contamination of an environment by persistent pesticides from all sources is a factor which should now be given greater weight by all concerned in proposals for the safe use of such chemicals. The aim should be to seek an order of priority for reduction of the total usage of such chemicals in agriculture without a serious setback to crop production.

Even if it were possible to withdraw the use of persistent organochlorine pesticides overnight, or if their use was abandoned completely, their presence in our immediate environment would continue, albeit to a lesser degree, because of the use of these chemicals in other countries. Imported foodstuffs from crops treated with these chemicals will continue to contain residues and for some years crops grown on treated soils will be similarly affected.

Dr Percy Stocks[16] who has been working with WHO on the relationship of smoking and solid-fuel air pollution has now put forward evidence supporting a hypothesis that both these forms of pollution, one personal and one general (and for many thus apparently additive), act by accelerating the final stages of cancerous growth of lungs and bronchus in those susceptibles who have reached an advanced point in the latent interval, and will explain many observed facts incompatible with the current view that everyone is liable to lung cancer.

When we observe the effects of the agents used in therapeutic treatment of the aberrations of Man's mind, we are conscious that this could easily become a pharmacological warfare against the integrity of his spirit as we witness evidence of misuse in an affluent world.

In conclusion, Man has at his disposal means of controlling his destiny on this planet so that he may have an abundant, creative and happy life, unmarred by hunger or malnutrition. But to secure this he must also learn to control himself in the midst of materials and facilities in excess of those adequate for his physiological and psychological health but which he is currently assembling in his affluent state.

REFERENCES

1. Autret, M., Pérricé, J., Sizaret, F. and Cresta, M., 1968. *Nutr. News Letter*, *6*, No. 4, p. 1. FAO, Rome.
2. Baird, D., Hytten, F. E. and Thomson, A. M., 1958. Age and human reproduction. *J. Obstet. Gyn. Brit. Emp.*, **66**, 865.

126 THE BIOLOGY OF AFFLUENCE

3. Barker, N., 1962. *Daily Mail*, June 5, 6, 8.
4. Crossman, R. H., 1965. *Planning for freedom*. Hamish Hamilton, London.
5. Cuthbertson, D. P., 1958. In 'The nutritional ages of man'. *Nutrition: past, present and future*, p. 38. Borden Company Foundation.
6. Eversley, D. E. C., 1969. In 'How many Britons is best?' *Nature*, **224**, 8.
7. Gabor, D., 1963. *Inventing the future*. Secker & Warburg, London.
8. Harrar, G., 1968. Strategy for the conquest of hunger. *Proceedings of a Symposium convened by the Rockefeller Foundation*, April 1-2, 1968. New York.
9. Hytten, F. E., 1955. Infant feeding. *Études néonatales*, **4**, 155.
10. Hytten, F. E. and Thomson, A. M., 1955. Clinical and chemical studies in human lactation. X. The maintenance of breast feeding. *Brit. Med. J.*, **2**, 232.
11. Lovell, B., 1969. The dangers of polluting the planets. *The Times*, Feb. 10th. London.
12. McGill, H. C. (ed.), 1968. The geographic pathology of atherosclerosis. *Lab. Invest.*, **18**, 463.
13. McMeekan, C. P., 1969. Inaugural Sir John Hammond lecture, March 31st.
14. Malthus, T. R., 1798. Essay on the principles of population as it affects the future improvement of society with remarks on the speculations of Mr. Godwin, Mr. Condorcet and other writers.
15. Nei, M., 1969. Gene duplication and nucleotide substitution in evolution. *Nature*, **221**, 40.
16. Stocks, P., 1967. Recent epidemiological studies of lung cancer, mortality, cigarette smoking and air pollution. *Brit. J. Cancer*, **20**, 595.
17. Tuck, R. H., 1969. Economics of protein production. Contribution to symposium *Proteins as human food*, 16th Easter School, University of Nottingham. March 30th-April 3rd, 1969.